THE
AZTECS

SUTTON POCKET HISTORIES

THE
AZTECS

BRENDA RALPH LEWIS

SUTTON PUBLISHING

First published in the United Kingdom in 1999 by
Sutton Publishing Limited · Phoenix Mill
Thrupp · Stroud · Gloucestershire · GL5 2BU

British Library Cataloguing in Publication Data
A catalogue record for this book is available from the British
Library.

ISBN 0-7509-2222-2

Cover illustration: Mask, representing the God Quetzalcoatl or
Tonatiuh, Aztec, *c.* 1500 (turquoise and shell on wood). (*Museum
of Mankind, London, UK/Bridgeman Art Library, London/New York*)

ALAN SUTTON™ and SUTTON™ are the
trade marks of Sutton Publishing Limited

Typeset in 11/14.5 pt Baskerville.
Typesetting and origination by
Sutton Publishing Limited.
Printed in Great Britain by
The Guernsey Press Company Limited,
Guernsey, Channel Islands.

Contents

List of Dates

1426	Death of Tezozómoc. His son Maxtla, a usurper, murders Chimalpopoca and Tlacateotl, ruler of Tlatelolco. Chimalpopoca's uncle, Itzcóatl, becomes fourth *tlatoani*.
1428	Death of Maxtla. Downfall of the Tepanec Empire. Itzcóatl forms Triple Alliance with Texcoco and Tacubans.
1440	Death of Itzcóatl. His nephew becomes fifth *tlatoani* as Montezuma I Ilhuacamina.
1446–50	Aztecs at war with Chalco.
1450–4	Famine in Tenochtitlan.
1458	Aztec conquest of Cempoala, Orizaba and other cities on the fertile coast of the Gulf of Mexico.
1468	Death of Montezuma I Ilhuacamina. His grandson Axayácatl succeeds as sixth *tlatoani*.
1473	Conquest of Tlatelolco by Tenochtitlan.
1478	Disastrous Aztec campaign against the Tarascans.
1481	Death of Axayácatl. His elder brother, Tizoc, becomes seventh *tlatoani*.
1486	Tizoc reputedly murdered. His younger brother, Ahuízotl, succeeds as eighth *tlatoani*.
1487	Temple of Huitzilopochtli in Tenochtitlan completed.
1487–8	Ahuízotl conquers Oztoma, Alahuiztla and Totonac Oaxaca.

1491–5	Aztec conquest of Pacific coast from Zacatula to Acapulco.
1492	**12 October**. Christopher Columbus lands on Guanahi (San Salvador, Bahamas)
1498	First European colonists settle on Española (Hispaniola). Ahuízotl conquers Tehuantepec (Isthmus of Panama).
1500	Amerigo Vespucci discovered that America is a continent. Ahuízotl conquers Soconusco. Tenochtitlan flooded.
1502	Death of Ahuízotl. His nephew, Montezuma II Xocoytzin, elected ninth *tlatoani*.
1499–1506	Spaniards explore the Atlantic coasts of central America and northern South America.
1504–7	Period of 'bad omens': Drought (1504) famine (1505) plague of rodents, eclipse of the Sun, earthquake (1507).
1509	Comet seen in Tenochtitlan. Spaniards occupy Jamaica.
1511	Spaniards colonise Cuba.
1512	Three earthquakes in Anahuac. Mysterious fire at temple of Huitzilopochtli.
1517	First Spanish expedition to Mexican mainland lands at Campeche (south-west of Gulf of Mexico).
1518	Second Spanish expedition lands at Cozumel, Yucatán.

1519	**12 March**. Hernán Cortés lands with 608 *conquistadores* at Tabasco (south east Mexico). 8 November. Cortés reaches Tenochtitlan. Takes Montezuma II prisoner.
1520	**2 May**. Cortés' rival, Panfilo de Narvaez, lands at Veracruz. Cortés leaves Tenochtitlan to deal with him. **25 June**. Five days after Cortés' return, Aztecs attack the Spaniards. **29 June**. Montezuma (previously deposed) dies from injuries. Cuitláhuac (brother of Montezuma) elected tenth *tlatoani*.
1520	**30 June** *Noche Triste*. Spaniards withdraw from Tenochtitlan to Tlaxcala, where Cortés plans his return. Smallpox epidemic in Tenochtitlan. Death of Cuitláhuac from smallpox. His nephew Quahtemoc (son of Ahuízotl) elected eleventh and last *tlatoani*.
1521	**28 April**. Siege of Tenochtitlan begins. **13 August**. Quahtemoc surrenders to Cortés. Ruins of Tenochtitlan fall to the Spaniards.

Introduction

On 8 November 1519 an army of about 400 Spaniards, exhausted from eleven punishing weeks battling high altitudes in the mountains of Mexico, rode along one of the three giant causeways which led across Lake Texcoco into the Aztec city of Tenochtitlan. Thousands of Aztecs were there to greet them, crammed along the causeway, on the *chinampas* – the floating garden islands anchored in the lake – and in a mass of small canoes.

What the Aztecs saw were pale-skinned men, strangely dressed, riding animals they had never seen before and carrying weapons which they already knew breathed fire and destruction on a scale not yet encountered in Anáhuac, the Valley of Mexico.

They had heard of this destructive capacity the previous March, not long after the Spaniards, who had reached Mexico from Cuba, arrived at Tabasco, which lay along the Rio Grijalva. After the Spaniards demonstrated their artillery, Aztec witnesses reported to Tenochtitlan: 'The great lombard gun expelled the shot which thundered as it went off. Something like a stone came out of it in a shower of fire and sparks . . . and the shot, which struck a mountain, knocked it to bits, dissolved it. It reduced a tree to sawdust. The tree disappeared as if it had been blown away. . . .' They went on: ' The animals they rode – they looked like deer – were as high as roof tops. And as to their war gear, it was all iron. They were iron. Their head pieces were of iron. Their swords, their crossbows, their shields, their lances were of iron. They covered their bodies completely, all except their faces. They were very white. Their eyes were like chalk. Their hair, on some it was yellow, on some it was black. They wore long beards; they were yellow, too.' (Sahagún (1978), Vol. 12)

What the Spaniards saw in Tenochtitlan was equally unfamiliar, but in their case, exciting. They were taken aback by the extent of this lake-built city, one of the largest in the known world, and above all by the opulence that surrounded them. As the *conquistador* Bernal Díaz del Castillo put it in his *The Conquest of New Spain* (*c.* 1562): 'When we saw all those cities and villages built in the water, and other great towns on dry land, and that straight and level causeway leading to Mexico [Tenochtitlan], we were astounded. . . . These great towns and pyramids and buildings rising from the water, all made of stone, seemed like an enchanted vision from the tale of Amadis. Indeed, some of our soldiers asked whether it was not all a dream.'

This emotional reaction was understandable. For the Spaniards, the last eleven weeks had been a mixture of extraordinary hardship endured in the hope of dazzling riches. They had seen the evidence at San Juan de Ulua, where objects of great beauty and value were laid before them. 'The first,' wrote Bernal Díaz, 'was a disk in the shape of the Sun, as big as a cartwheel and made of very fine gold. It was a marvellous thing, engraved with many sorts of figures and, as those who afterwards weighed it reported, was worth more than 10,000 pesos. There was another, larger, disk of brightly shining silver in the shape of the moon . . . and this was worth a great deal, for it was very heavy. . . .'

These treasures were only two among the mass of wealth from the empire ruled by the *tlatoani* ('He who Speaks' or Great Speaker) Montezuma II Xoyoctzin. Aztec observers later recorded the

Spaniards' reactions. 'They seized upon the gold as if they were monkeys, their faces gleaming. For clearly their thirst for gold was insatiable; they starved for it; they lusted for it; they wanted to stuff themselves with it as if they were pigs.' (Sahagún (1978), Vol. 12)

However, the Spaniards were treated with much more honour than this contemptuous description implies. Montezuma Xoyoctzin had given orders that the Spaniards were to be welcomed, housed, nourished and even pampered. It was a curious reaction from a ruler whose personal instincts were despotic, and whose empire, created by war, brutally exploited its subject Mixtec, Zapotec, Maya and other peoples. Montezuma, however, was under the impression that the Spaniards were gods and that their leader, Hernán Cortés, was the reincarnation of Quetzalcoatl, the Plumed Serpent, and the god-king of his ancestors, the Toltecs. The return of Quetzalcoatl from the exile which had begun with the fall of the Toltec capital, Tula, in 1168, had long been predicted. Quite possibly, Spanish accounts exploited the return of Quetzalcoatl for Spanish purposes. It has also been suggested that the story was invented by the *tetecuhtin*, the Aztec nobility, to make Montezuma's frightened reactions seem rational.

However it came about, though, this was the greatest and most fatal case of mistaken identity in history, and prefigured the most disastrous clash of cultures to occur in the 400 years between the sixteenth and the nineteenth centuries, which saw the creation of European empires overseas. As empire-builders, the Spaniards had a different ethos from the British, French or Dutch. These other Europeans ventured abroad mainly for trade, settlement and exploitation of the land, its resources and the local labour. The Spaniards came for much more complex reasons. One, certainly, was gold and all the other forms of wealth to be found in America, but the *conquistadores* also sought estates and honours not available in Spain to men of their humble birth. Spaniards were avid, too, for discovery and adventure, and for converts to Christianity.

For all their well-documented cruelties and their boundless greed, the Spaniards were more enterprising, more intellectual and more imaginative than any other Europeans bent on empire. Their enterprise in Mexico proved typical of what they were prepared to endure in order to reach their goals. There, they faced the steaming heat of the coastal plain, the thick, tangled forests, and the perilous, narrow mountain passes where nights were fearsomely cold and the air so thin that it was difficult to breathe, let alone move. Many died before they had a chance to reach Tenochtitlan, in accidents in the mountains, at the hands of hostile tribesmen or from sheer exhaustion. Elsewhere in America, Spaniards survived jungles, fast-flowing rivers, unhealthy swamps, broiling temperatures and ferocious natives far less welcoming than the Aztecs.

Spaniards explored, they observed, they researched and above all, they recorded, leaving behind the most comprehensive coverage of foreign territory compiled by Europeans anywhere in the world. However, just as the identification of Cortés with the returned god Quetzalcoatl has to be treated with a certain amount of caution, a similar proviso applies when judging the conquerors' accounts of the conquered. In his five letters to King Charles of Spain Cortés may have exaggerated the size and power of the Aztec towns and cities in order to magnify his own achievement in conquering them.

Together with other Spanish writers, he may also have added lurid colour to his picture of the Aztec religion and the extent of its human sacrifice, so that the need for Christianity to save such savages from their own demoniac doings would seem all the more urgent.

Much remains obscure or unknown about the Aztecs and their world, though since the 1970s archaeology has done a great deal to illuminate the picture (Smith, pp. 3–6). Even so, it is true that without venturers like Bernal Díaz, who wrote the first, definitive Spanish account of the conquest of Mexico, or the priests Fray Bernardino de Sahagún and Fray Diego Durán – the most accurate and impartial of observers – far less would be known of pre-Hispanic Mexico, its ethnology, government, history, plant and animal life, theology, cosmology, philosophy, mythology and medicine.

Primarily, of course, the priests came to save souls for Christ. In America, they found a whole continent full of pagan 'deviants', ripe for conversion and with rites and practices that the priests found both horrendous and disgusting. So it appeared on the surface, for besides human sacrifice there was cannibalism, as bodies were divided up for eating as part of the ceremony. However, from the Aztec point of view, sacrifice – which also included maize, vegetables, birds and small animals – was a natural response to the dangerous volcanic environment of the Valley of Mexico. The suffering, forgiving god of Christianity was utterly alien to them when their own deities were malign, terrifying figures who made the twin volcanoes Popacatépetl and Iaxtacchuatl shake and breathe fire, and had to be constantly mollified to keep them from destroying the world.

To Europeans, such atavistic beliefs sat strangely with other features of a civilisation that could boast remarkable achievements in astronomy, mathematics, art, sculpture, weaving, metalwork, music and architecture. In this context, Aztec Mexico was in some ways superior to contemporary Europe. For instance, using only the naked eye, the Aztec astronomer-priests could chart planetary movements and record them by means of geometric and other mathematical symbols. Tenochtitlan, together with its sister-city Tlatelolco, was reckoned to be five times larger than contemporary London. The Aztec capital featured huge stone palaces, giant stepped pyramids, the *teocalli* or twin temples 30 metres high, and a vista of flat-roofed buildings all constructed, Venice-like, on Lake Texcoco and joined to the shore by huge causeways, each over 4 km long. For a culture which used no metal implements or working animals, Tenochtitlan-Tlatelolco was a dazzling achievement.

In the event, however, developments which had *not* taken place in ancient America proved much more crucial than those that had. Metals were not used for weapons, and the Aztecs had nothing to match the fine-tempered steel of the Spaniards' superlative swords. Neither had they discovered gunpowder, which had already seen action in European wars for nearly 200 years. The Aztecs had no horses for transport in war or trade, and as a result these strange animals with Spaniards on their backs inspired awe and terror. Perhaps most vital of all, the individuality which powered the Spanish will had no place in conformist Aztec minds, which placed community and state before self, and the gods before everything. Long before the two sides met, therefore, the balance was heavily weighted one way and there could, in consequence, be only one, fatal, outcome.

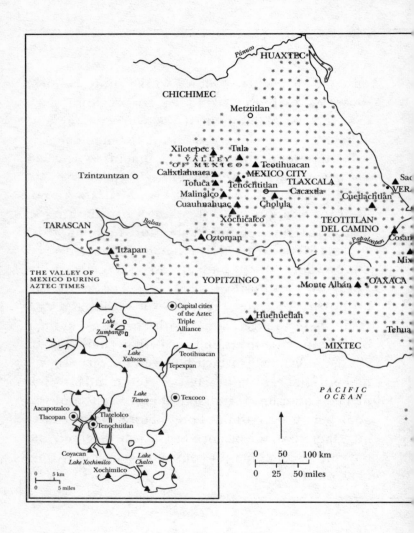

THE VALLEY OF
MEXICO DURING
AZTEC TIMES

F OF MEXICO

YUCATAN
PENINSULA

Xicallanco

Candelaria

Grijalva

Usumacinta

cos

CARIBBEAN
SEA

Ulúa

*Xoconoxco ▲

tec Empire at AD 1521

ttlements and garrison

archaeological sites

n city

ONE

Beginnings

In ancient Mesoamerica, history tended to be god-led and so became bound up in myth and legend. The Aztecs' history was no exception. For them, divine will was paramount and became the focus of many powerful superstitions. Divine intervention is therefore a prominent theme of the *Tira de la Peregrinación*, also known as the Codex Boturini, a 549 cm long strip of fig-tree bark of some twenty-one pages, now in the Mexican National Museum of Anthropology in Mexico City. This recounts the beginnings of the Aztec nation in a series of painted panels.

According to the *Tira*, the Aztecs came upon a carved stone head of the god Huitzilopochtli, Humming Bird of the South or Hummingbird on the Left, which emitted a curious whistling sound. Huitzilopochtli promised that if the Aztecs were loyal to him, and carried the stone head with them

1

on their future wanderings, he would give them a sign when they reached their place of permanent settlement. Afterwards, he would make them masters of all Mexico.

Subsequently, the Aztecs left their homeland of Aztlan and settled for a time at the Seven Caves, a legendary locale which also served in other mythologies as the starting point for other Mesoamerican tribes with a great future before them. Here, though, the Aztecs made a grave mistake. They cut down a sacred tree, greatly angering Huitzilopochtli, who punished them with poverty and put an indeterminate length of time on their wanderings.

By contrast, the account of ancient Aztec history set down in 1609 by Hernando Alvarez Tezozómoc, a grandson of Montezuma Xocoytzin, *begins* at the Seven Caves. According to Tezozómoc, the earliest forebears of the Aztecs came into being in the bowels of the earth, before passing through the caves and emerging to people Aztlan from Chicomoztoc, a huge rock with 'holes in seven sides; . . . that was a fearsome place, for there abounded the countless wild beasts established in the area; bears, tigers, pumas, serpents; and it is full of thorns, of sweet agave and of pastures; and being thus very far off, no one still knew later where it was.' (Tezozómoc, p. 17)

Modern anthropology, however, has revealed a less intimate connection between the Aztecs and the soil of America, where there was no human life before Ice Age hunters began to wander across the land bridge, now covered by the Bering Strait, which led from eastern Siberia into present-day Alaska. Following the herds of animals on which they lived, the hunters arrived in America between 200 and 300 centuries ago. Over time, America's first inhabitants spread across the twin continents, and along the way discovered how to grow maize, which yielded copious crops and enabled settled farming communities. The migrations, however, persisted. In Mexico, the nomads were known as Chichimecs, 'sons of the dog', and included the Aztecs among many other peoples who came from the north and ultimately settled in the Valley of Mexico. Some Chichimecs lived in one place for several years before moving on and this pattern marked the early centuries of Aztec history. In AD 1111, according to some reckonings, though the *Tira* names the year as 1168, the Aztecs left Aztlan and travelled to Mexico, waiting for the sign Huitzilopochtli had promised them. At some time during their peregrinations, they learned of the sacrifices their god had ordained. The *Tira* relates how they came upon three bodies lying on cacti with their chests ripped open and their hearts missing. At this juncture, more than two centuries were to pass before the Aztecs reached Lake Texcoco, their final place of settlement. In the interim, their day-to-day existence depended on hunting deer, rabbits, birds and snakes. From time to time, they remained in one place long enough to grow crops.

In about 1163, the Aztecs came to Coatepec, which was probably near Tula. Here, settlement became sufficiently permanent for the Aztecs to dam the nearby river and to enjoy for some time a plentiful food supply. The idea that Coatepec could be the Aztecs' final home was, however, quashed by Huitzilopochtli. Coatepec became unlivable after he ordered the destruction of the dam which rendered the land barren and caused the death or departure of its animal life. The Aztecs packed up and moved on, and in about 1168, reached Tula, the Toltec capital, which lay only some 64 km from Lake Texcoco and the future site of Tenochtitlan. That same year, the Toltecs' empire, together with their city, succumbed to attacks by Chichimecs who may have included the Aztecs. This disintegration of the mightiest power in Mexico left a power vacuum which the Aztecs, who might have served as military aides to the Toltecs, would one day fill. However, despite the proximity of their final destination, the Aztecs had a great deal more wandering to do.

The year 1299 found them at Chapultepec, a former Toltec stronghold, which now lay in the land of the Tepanecs, one of two great powers in the Valley of Mexico. At this time, the Valley was a cauldron of rivalry and enmity, and here the Aztecs, still poor and powerless, were not made welcome. Neighbouring tribes, including the Tepanecs, attacked them, driving them from Chapultepec in 1315 and again, after a brief return, in 1319.

At this nadir of their fortunes, the Aztecs appealed to Coxcoxtli, one of the rulers of Culhuacan on the eastern shore of Lake Texcoco, to the south-west of Chapultepec. He allowed them to settle at Tizaapan, 10 km west of Culhuacan. Tizaapan, however, was a fearful place and the Aztecs were not expected to survive among the vistas of volcanic rock and an environment thickly infested with poisonous serpents and other reptiles.

Evidently, Coxcoxtli had no great opinion of the wretched refugees. When told that the Aztecs had moved in at Tizaapan, he said: 'It is good, for they are no true people, but great villains, and perhaps they will perish there, eaten by the serpents . . . ' (Tezozómoc, pp. 49–51). The Aztecs, however, confounded him. They not only survived, reputedly roasting and eating the serpents in the process, they so impressed the Culhua that they were allowed to trade and intermarry and serve as mercenaries in Culhua wars. In one conflict fought against nearby Xochimilco, the Aztecs, armed with stone knives and wooden clubs, not only prevailed, but returned to Culhua with hundreds of severed ears in baskets which they carried on their backs. These they poured out in front of a horrified Coxcoxtli to prove how many men they had killed (Anales de Tlatelolco, p. 41).

The Culhua reaction was disgust and dismay at the bloodthirsty potential of their mercenaries. Subsequently, the Aztecs confirmed this opinion when at Huitzilopochtli's bidding, they killed and flayed a young Culhuacan princess who was, ostensibly, to become the wife of their god. The Aztecs then invited her father, Achitometl, to the wedding, where he came across a priest wearing her skin.

Achitometl, of course, demanded vengeance and yet again the Aztecs were ejected. They escaped to Acatzintlan on the shore of the Lake Texcoco, where the water was shallow enough for them to cross. After reaching a small island in the lake, 'they took shelter among the reeds and rushes, where they passed the night in great anguish and sore affliction, with their women and children still crying and begging that they should be left to die there, as they could bear no more travails' (Durán, Vol. 2, p. 43).

Fortunately for these ferocious, if suffering, people their wanderings were at an end. As the *Tira* records, Huitzilopochtli had decreed that the Aztecs' final destination would be at a spot where they came upon an eagle – their god, metamorphosed – perched on a cactus plant. Shortly after the Aztecs reached the island, they discovered a stream full of red and blue water. These were their symbolic colours of victory. Following the water to its source beneath a rock, the Aztecs found a cactus, and on the cactus, a white eagle with a serpent gripped in its talons. This, the Aztec priests declared, was the long-awaited sign from Huitzilopochtli. This was the place the god had named Tenochtitlan, 'the Place of the Fruit of the Cactus' or 'Cactus Rock'. The year, Two House in the Aztec calendar, was equivalent to 1325 in Aztec reckoning or 1345 in Culhua-Texcocan reckoning.

The site of the great city which was to amaze the Spaniards was, at this stage, uninviting but at least viable. It was small, marshy and full of reeds, but food, in the form of fish and birds, was plentiful. Land area fit for cultivation was limited, but Aztec ingenuity increased its potential with the building of *chinampas* – artificial islands made from water plants and mud dredged from the bottom of the lake and secured in place by woven reed walls. There were few raw materials but the site was easy to defend, an important advantage when the Valley of Mexico was such a nest of enemies.

A sister-city, Tlatelolco, was founded in about 1358, and in time became a great commercial centre whose rich and extensive market was later described in detail by Bernal Diáz del Castillo. Much later, the merchants of Tlatelolco helped fuel the campaigns of conquest launched from Tenochtitlan by combining trading missions with spying and reconnaissance and, in some cases, initiating warfare themselves.

Immediately after the founding of the lake-borne city, the most prominent Aztec leader was Tenochtli, or Tenoch. Tenochtli was a possibly legendary figure, one of four priest-rulers instrumental in preserving the Aztecs during the trials they endured – or, according to one's point of view, brought upon themselves – in Culhuacan. The principle functions of the Aztec state were divided among these priest-rulers, who were appointed by popular choice. The province of the High Priest was religious observance, there was a Controller of Markets, and a military leader later known as the *Cihuacóatl* or Serpent Woman, who was in fact a man. Tenochtli, it appears, was the Speaker, not to be confused with the *tlatoani*, the Great Speaker of later Aztec history. However, this distinction does not appear to have applied to Tenochtli, who is depicted as a powerful, if not all-powerful, ruling figure in the Codex Mendoza (*c.* 1541/2), the Aztec painted manuscript specially prepared for the first Viceroy of New Spain, Don Antonio de Mendoza. In the Codex, Tenochtli is shown seated on a palm-leaf mat, denoting power, and appears complete with blue tongue, indicating authority, and speech-glyph representing his role in Aztec affairs. (Codex Mendoza, p. 19) However, the same page in the Codex also includes ten other leaders and it was possible that, in its earliest days, Tenochtitlan was controlled by a committee, as it were, of up to thirteen members.

Tenochtli is said to have died about twenty-five years after Tenochtitlan was founded and no priest-ruler was chosen to take his place. Instead, the Aztecs decided on a form of monarchy and sought a candidate in Culhuacan. Acamapichtli, the prince chosen in 1372, as the first official *tlatoani* was the product of Aztec-Culhua intermarriage. Acamapichtli's father was an Aztec *tecuhtli* and his mother was a princess, the daughter of the Culhua ruler. This first *tlatoani* was a shrewd choice. Acamapichtli represented not only a blood tie with the Culhua, the second most powerful people in the Valley of Mexico after the Tepanecs, but was said to be descended from the mighty warrior Toltecs. Acamapichtli, therefore, gave the Aztecs a cachet they had never previously enjoyed.

Tlatelolco, too, acquired its first monarch at the same time as Tenochtitlan in the person of

Cuacuapitzhuac, whose father was the formidable Tezozómoc of Azcapotzalco, founder of the Tepanec Empire. Tezozómoc was a ruler of extraordinary diplomatic skill and military prowess and his realm, which covered almost the whole Valley of Mexico, was all the more stable because of his great longevity: he reigned for an extraordinary fifty years, until his death in 1426. He outlived both Acamapichtli, who died in 1391, and the next two *tlatoani*, as well as his son, who died in 1407. Throughout their reigns, in fact, the ruthless, manipulative Tezozómoc held Acamapichtli and Cuacaupitzahuac in thrall as his vassals and tributaries of the Tepanec state (Durán, Vol. 12, p. 58).

Even so, despite the pressures of his subordinate status, Acamapichtli achieved a great deal in his nineteen years as *tlatoani*. Tenochtitlan, which had started as a collection of simple reed huts, began to attain some of its later grandeur, as it acquired some stone buildings and the character of a seat of government. The city still had a very long way to go before it would become the dazzling metropolis the Spaniards saw: the giant causeways, for instance, had yet to be built. All the same, the reign of

Acamapichtli saw the start of urban organisation. In Tenochtitlan the land area was divided into four districts, whose various sub-districts, portioned out among fifteen or twenty *calpulli* (clans), possessed their own gods and temples.

On a personal level, Acamapichtli carried out a duty incumbent on all founders of royal houses: he married well, and more than once. His first wife, Ilancuetl, who came from Culhuacan, was herself of royal blood and though she had no children she was apparently a strong political influence in the nascent ruling house in Tenochtitlan. Acamapichtli's offspring were provided by other, secondary wives – he seems to have married up to twenty of them – who were probably the daughters of *calpulli* leaders. In this way, the first *tlatoani* anchored the royal house to the Aztec people, providing a class of interrelated nobles which was unlikely to run out of legitimate successors.

Acamapichtli's reign saw, too, the first stirrings of the mighty military machine which would one day enable Tenochtitlan to dominate an empire of some 12 million subjects, 250,000 sq km and 38 provinces in size, stretching from the Gulf of Mexico to the shores of the Pacific. However, the Aztecs were still essentially mercenaries at this period, and in the reign of Acamapichtli the major share of any spoils belonged not to them, but to their lords, the Tepanecs.

In this context, some Aztec victories listed as 'conquests' might have been no more than successful raids. The Aztecs conducted some campaigns on their own behalf and Acamapichtli was credited with the capture of four large towns around Lake Texcoco, including Cuernavaca and Xochimilco; nevertheless, the Tepanecs could legitimately claim the tribute later forced from the inhabitants. The situation was much the same at the start of a long conflict with Chalco that began in about 1375, not long after Acamapichtli was elected, when the Aztecs were participating as auxiliaries. However, as the war continued, with intervals of truce, the Aztecs took on the role of prime movers and hostilities ended with a triumph of their own in 1465.

By then, the peoples of the valley were in no doubt that the pariahs who had once been used and abused had become a ruthless, expansionist power greatly to be feared and often fatal to resist.

TWO

Building an Empire

Before he died in 1391, Acamapichtli expressed one great regret: that he had not been able to free Tenochtitlan from 'servitude and tribute' to the Tepanecs. However, Acamapichtli's successor, his son Huitzilíhuitl, intended to create the conditions to make this possible. On his election, Huitzilíhuitl became High Priest and Commander-Chief of the Aztecs, as well as political leader. And like his father, those who chose him, the most prominent among them the leaders of the four main *calpulli*, left the new *tlatoani* in no doubt about the onerous nature of his position. 'Valiant young man, our king and lord,' he was told, 'do not be dismayed or lose heart on account of the new charge that has been laid upon you, in that you should protect the land and water of your new kingdom. . . . Do not think that you are chosen in order to rest, but to work' (Durán, Vol. 2, p. 62).

This was likely to be the last time Huitzilíhuitl would be addressed in such familiar terms. The office of *tlatoani* not only made its holder divine, it translated him into the formalised life the Aztecs considered appropriate for a god. He was treated with the utmost awe and deference. Wherever he walked, the ground upon which he trod was swept beforehand. No one was allowed to look him in the face, touch him, see him eat, or, except in the case of his closest advisers, talk directly to him or hear him speak.

Huitzilíhuitl, however, had a healthy sense of realism which transcended ceremonials. He knew he must reinforce his position to have the best chance of success and expand the influence of the still quite small Aztec state. Huitzilíhuitl's first move was typical of a minor, but ambitious, monarch: after his first wife, a Tacuban princess died, he made an advantageous second marriage with a daughter of the Tepanec ruler Tezozómoc, so elevating the Aztec royal house to a position almost on a par with that of its overlords. This rise in status was reinforced when a son, Chimalpopoca, was born in about about 1397 and led, in time, to a lessening of the tribute the Tepanecs required from the Aztecs. This move was vigorously opposed by members of the Tepanec ruling council. To them, reducing the tribute would compound Aztec ambitions and might one day lead to a direct challenge to Tepanec control.

Huitzilíhuitl's hidden agenda came under even more suspicion when, after his second wife died in about 1406, the *tlatoani* married Miahuaxihuitl, a Tlahuica princess from Cuernavaca, a city in south-central Mexico then known as Cuauhnáhuac. This third union expanded Huitzilíhuitl's territorial influence in the south. At this juncture, though, he was still bound to the mercenary services he owed the Tepanecs and in 1398 had received some valuable spoils of war: territory at Xaltocan, north of the Valley of Mexico. Xaltocan boasted a prize commodity scarce in Tenochtitlan – agricultural land.

However, the ongoing struggle against Chalco yielded not advantage, but a humiliating lesson possibly aimed at curbing growing Aztec self-confidence. In 1411 the Aztecs captured Chalco and installed their own rulers, but were prevented from consolidating their triumph by an alliance which included the Tepanecs. Not long afterwards, events proved that even the mighty Tezozómoc did not have total control of Tepanec policies. He tended to be indulgent towards his grandson, Chimalpopoca, who succeeded his father in 1415. Tezozómoc willingly came to the new *tlatoani*'s aid when the degraded water supply at Tenochtitlan called for an aqueduct and the materials to build it. The furore of objection this caused in Azcapotzalco was still going on when Tezozómoc died in 1426 and, reputedly, contributed to his death (Tezozómoc, pp. 23–4).

With this, the family favour that Chimalpopoca had enjoyed was gone and his new vulnerability became grimly apparent when Tezozómoc's son Maxtla succeeded his father as Tepanec ruler after murdering the true heir, his elder brother Tayauh. Determined to curb the rising power of the Aztecs, Maxtla added Chimalpopoca and Tlacateotl, ruler of Tlatelolco, to his hit list. In 1426 in Tenochtitlan Chimalpopoca was seized by assassins, thrust into a cage and killed. Tlacateotl was pursued as he tried to escape and was drowned when his canoe was sunk in the deepest part of Lake Texcoco (Ixlilxóchitl, Vol. 2, p. 120).

A more elaborate account has suggested that Chimalpopoca had decided to commit suicide to cheat Maxtla of his revenge, and offered himself as a human sacrifice to the Aztec priests. However, Maxtla's assassins had got there first. Before the sacrifice could take place, they seized the *tlatoani*, and carried him off in the cage for disposal. Other culprits named in the untimely death of Chimalpopoca were his successor, his uncle Itzcóatl, who, it was rumoured, disposed of the third *tlatoani* because of his subservient attitude towards the Tepanecs.

Itzcóatl succeeded his luckless nephew as fourth *tlatoani* and joined forces with another nemesis, Nezahualcóyotl of Texcoco. As a young boy Nezahualcóyotl had seen his father Ixlilxóchitl, the Texcocan ruler, killed by Tepanecs during a campaign against his city. Maxtla attempted several times to have Nezahualcóyotl killed, but the Texcocan appeared to have charmed life and eluded his pursuers every time. Legends about Nezahualcóyotl suggested that he was a descendant of Huitzilopochtli and of Tezcatlipoca, god of the night sky. His more mundane ancestry traces his descent from an Aztec royal mother. In 1428, by which time he had dislodged the Tepanecs from Texcoco and retrieved his realm, Nezahualcóyotl went to the aid of Tenochtitlan, then being besieged by the dastardly Maxtla.

Ultimately, Maxtla was faced with an alliance of Tenochtitlan, Texcoco, a group of dissident Tepanecs in Tacuba, Huexotzingo and Tlaxcala. The threat was so great that Maxtla abandoned his siege of Tenochtitlan and fell back on Azcapotzalco and its fortifications. The allies soon came after him. They converged on Azcapotzalco, and after initial violent fighting, laid siege to the Tepanec capital. The defenders were soon reduced to starvation and within four months, Maxtla found himself at the mercy of the Aztecs and their Texcocan allies.

In dealing with, or rather disposing of, Maxtla, the victors had the assistance of the craven Tepanec rulers: 'The leaders of Azcapotzalco, seeing that they were lost, sought out their king, who went to hide in a *temazcal* which stood behind a garden, and which is a bath. With many insults they dragged him before Nezahualcóyotl, saying that . . . had it not been for Maxtla and his forebears, who had always been inclined towards tyranny, the state would not have suffered such wars and casualties.' Subsequently, Nezahualcóyotl exacted his personal revenge by cutting out Maxtla's heart and scattering his blood to the four points of the compass.

With this great victory, which felled the greatest single power in the Valley of Mexico, the ground was cleared for the expansionist ambitions of the Aztecs. They were already a nascent imperialist power. Their army was experienced in long-range war and their officials at gathering tribute and controlling vassals. Their economy was burgeoning and the merchants of Tlatelolco were boosting their prosperity with trade in plumes, jewels and other luxuries. In addition, the Aztec agricultural base was flourishing, with the fertile *chinampas* dotting the lake and a mass of canoes on lucrative business navigating the intersecting canals.

Furthermore, Tenochtitlan was now controlled by a strong team. The 46-year-old Itzcóatl was a mature, strong-arm *tlatoani* who aimed to take advantage of the first real independence the Aztecs had enjoyed since leaving Aztlan. He was backed by two of his nephews, both of them considerable personalities in their own right. The elder, Montezuma Ilhuacamina, had proved himself as a military leader in the Tepanec war. The younger, Montezuma's brother Tlacaélel, became the first *Cihuacóatl*, or Serpent

Woman, a position second only to that of the *tlatoani* himself. It was, apparently, Tlacaélel who persuaded Itzcóatl to destroy the records of Aztec history up to his time and revise them in more glorious guise, complete with a divine destiny, as befitted the first *tlatoani* of the Aztecs to be his own man.

As such, Itzcóatl was canny enough to realise that his best chance of dominating the mass of contentious peoples inhabiting the Valley of Mexico was to do so in harness with others. This was why he formed the Triple Alliance with Nezahualcóyotl, 'Ruler of the Acolhuas' to the east of Lake Texcoco and the 'Ruler of the Tepanecs' based at Tacuba. Itzcóatl, the senior partner, styled himself 'Ruler of the Culhua' and set about mopping up the remnants of the Tepanec Empire – first Coyoacan, next Xochimilco, then Cuitláhuac and later Cuernavaca and other cities close by. In each case, as was the custom in Mesoamerican wars, a pretext was found to initiate proceedings. This usually involved one side making demands, some of them quite trivial, which the other was bound to refuse. After their defeat, the lands and labour of the vanquished would be exploited by their conquerors. For instance, labourers from Xochimilco were put to work on building the first of the giant causeways linking Tenochtitlan to the lake shore.

Itzcóatl died in 1440, not long after the capture of Cuitláhuac, leaving the valley well consolidated in Aztec hands and the machinery of Tenochtitlan poised for yet more expansion. His elder nephew, later styled as Montezuma I Ilhuacamina, was elected to succeed him. As was only fitting for the ruler of the Valley of Mexico, the fifth *tlatoani*'s coronation was a splendid affair, accompanied by several days and nights of celebration, the giving of gifts and acts of charity towards the poor of Tenochtitlan. The human sacrifices made as part of the celebrations had been obtained in the customary war, in this case with Chalco, with which Montezuma I had inaugurated his reign (Codex Ramírez, p. 79). It was a shrewd choice: the Chalcoans represented the last remaining mote in the eye of total Aztec supremacy which had swept all the other peoples surrounding the valley under their dominion.

Chalco was a tough opponent: proud, resourceful, and well equipped. Its army was, in fact, so large that Aztec agents reconnoitring the border reported that it filled an entire plain. The Aztecs nevertheless prevailed, capturing 500 prisoners for their sacrificial altars. However, though defeated, Chalco had not been entirely subdued when the greatest crisis the Aztecs had so far faced occurred in Tenochtitlan: a serious famine which followed a series of environmental disasters. First, there was a plague of locusts in 1446, then the city was flooded by the rising waters of Lake Texcoco. A dam nearly 15 km long and built of huge stone slabs was constructed to hold back further flooding, but bad harvests, the first in 1450, and unusually heavy snowfalls which destroyed the vital maize crops, compounded the catastrophe. Stores laid by as an emergency food supply ran out when year after year there were fresh crop failures with more early frosts, drought and the destruction of seed for future planting.

This was when famine descended like a miasma on the valley, killing the elderly, shrivelling the young with hunger and bringing in the vultures, which hovered about in the expectation of corpses. Thus afflicted, the Aztecs in Tenochtitlan took extreme measures in order to survive. Some sold themselves as slaves to the coastal peoples down on the Gulf of Mexico. Others sold their children in exchange for maize, a boy meriting 500 cobs, a girl 400.

Eventually, in 1454, Montezuma Ilhuacamina, was forced to admit defeat in the face of calamity. 'All supplies are now consumed,' he told the Aztecs. 'All that remains is to say that the Lord of the Heavens wills that each one of you should now seek his own remedy.' (Durán, Vol. 2, p. 243) Fortunately, the remedy was at hand. Copious rains fell in 1455, producing harvests in an abundance not seen for years. The crisis was over, but the lessons had been learned. Such a terrible event must never happen again. In consequence, the future spread of empire was directed towards those east coast areas unaffected by the famine which, environmentally, were much more clement than the rocky, volcanic valley of the Mexican plateau. There, nearly 2,500 metres up in the mountains, aridisols meant that vegetation was sparse and fertility had to be coaxed from the soil through extensive irrigation systems. By contrast, in the tropical lowlands that swept down to the gulf, nature's bounty burgeoned, providing fruits, vegetables and staple crops in plenty, while the forests teemed with plant and animal life.

The need to ensure survival was not the only motive
to fuel the post-famine campaigns of Montezuma
Ilhuacamina. This other, fertile world by the sea also
offered great mineral wealth and a multiplicity of
birds – parrots, parakeets, macaws, toucans, and the
gorgeous *quetzal* – which meant a copious supply of
the brilliant feathers so important as status symbols
for the military and nobility in Tenochtitlan.

The initial Aztec drive, which began in 1458,
headed south-east, towards Coixlahuaca, an
important Mixtec commercial hub which was the
centre of its own empire and could prove the
springboard for further conquests in the region.
This campaign was unlike any other the Aztecs and
their allies had yet attempted, with great distances to
be covered on foot and a mass of food, tents,
weaponry and other supplies needed for the long
journey so far from home. When eventually
Coixlahuaca came under attack, the city easily
succumbed to Aztec force, and the ritual which
signified victory was performed, with the burning of
the chief Mixtec temple. The Lord of Coixlahuaca,
Atonal, was strangled, or so he appears in the Codex
Mendoza, with a rope around his neck while, nearby,
his temple is ablaze (Codex Mendoza, p. 26).

The conquest of the Coixlahuaca secured the Aztec rear for their next campaign, eastwards towards the gulf coast, with Cempoala as the first target. The Tlaxcalans, deadly enemies of the Aztecs, encouraged the local Totonacs to resist, but this did nothing to divert the advance of the Aztecs and their allies against, first, Orizaba and later, the forces of other coastal cities. As the Aztecs made a bloody progress through Totonac country, terrified villagers went into hiding with their animals and food supplies.

Ultimately, their territory was added to Montezuma Ilhuacamina's realm. So were the lands of the Huaxtecs north of the coastal strip and Tepeaca, south of Tlaxcala, which lay along the Aztec routes to their new domains. By 1465 Chalco had been added to the tributary roll, when their final defeat, postponed by the great famine, was at last accomplished.

The now extensive empire won by Montezuma Ilhuacamina, and extended by later Aztec rulers, was not based on acquiring territory, establishing provincial bureaucracies or unseating local rulers: they were usually allowed to remain in charge subject to the continuance of tribute to Tenochtitlan.

This made the empire a tribute-gathering enterprise, which brought with it vast wealth in foodstuffs, textiles, feathers, gold and precious stones together with an ongoing supply of labourers, slaves, military auxiliaries and human sacrifices.

Montezuma Ilhuacamina's campaigns of imperial conquest ended in 1466, which gave him only two years to enjoy the heady fruits of imperial success. In that brief time, however, he proceeded in the manner common among emperors, building great monuments and structures to serve as a metaphor for his greatness. His prime construction was a temple to Huitzilopochtli, for which he summoned materials, supplies and labour from his newly subjected domains. It was a magnificent, brilliantly painted construction, with 360 steps leading to the figure of the god at the summit. Another monument was a great round stone carved with images recounting his many conquests, and another the creation of beautiful gardens with waterfalls, reservoirs and a mass of trees and plants specially brought to the valley from the tropical coastlands. Finally, before he died in 1468, Montezuma Ilhuacamina ordered the carving of twin statues, one of himself, the other of his brother Tlacaélel, from the rock of the hill at Chapultepec.

Montezuma Ilhuacamina appears to have been very conscious of his own lustre as an imperial *tlatoani*. This sense of status was evident in laws setting out the boundaries of class in Aztec society in ways which boosted the ruling élite. The *tlatoani*, Montezuma decreed, would appear in public only on the most important occasions. Only the *tlatoani* and his chief minister, the Serpent Woman, could wear fine sandals inside the royal palace. Only the *tetecuhtin* (the nobility) could wear cotton clothing, or lip, ear and nose plugs of gold and precious stones, and together with valiant warriors, were the only ones permitted to live in houses with a second storey.

Montezuma Ilhuacamina's successor, his inexperienced grandson Axayácatl, inherited this grandeur when he was chosen *tlatoani* at the age of nineteen, but though his reign had its glories, it also featured setbacks which took some of the shine from the imperial mystique. Axayácatl initiated his reign in the usual manner, first with a campaign against rebellion in Cotaxtla and later, in 1473, in a struggle much nearer home.

Tenochtitlan's twin city, Tlatelolco, had become a very powerful foundation, as the commercial centre of Aztec life and the base for merchants who had blazed the trail of empire across Mexico. By 1473, however, a certain rivalry had built up between the two cities and came to its crux through a royal family quarrel, after the ruler of Tlatelolco, Moquihuix, misused his wife, Axayácatl's sister, and took to cavorting with his concubines. Outraged, Axayácatl gave notice of his preparations for war by sending his brother-in-law the ritual feathers, together with sword and shield. Moquihuix made the first move, advancing towards Tenochtitlan, but was forced to retreat and was pursued into Tlatelolco, where Axayáctl laid him under siege in the market-place. Retiring to the great pyramid temple of Tlatelolco, Moquihuix vowed to fight to the death, a fate which shortly overtook him when Axayácatl's forces swarmed up the steps and threw him from the top of the temple.

Honour apparently satisfied, Axayácatl ordered an end to the fighting, and proceeded to treat the Tlatelolcoans like defeated enemies. He demanded tribute, slaves for sacrifice, the handing over of large tracts of land and most onerous of all, denied them their own temple to Huitzilopochtli. Tlatelolco was then pillaged. The city was never independent again, and rule from Tenochtitlan was exercised by a military governor. Fortunately the dynastic feud did not cause a split in the Triple Alliance and Tenochtitlan emerged from this brief, but vicious civil war more powerful in the valley than ever before.

Next, in 1474, Axayácatl took advantage of a feud over tribute between the rulers of Toluca and Tenancingo, in which he was called upon to arbitrate, to make both of them tributaries of Tenochtitlan. This affair had important repercussions. The new Aztec territories afforded protection against the dangerous Tarascans, whose territory lay beyond Toluca. Axayácatl's return to Tenochtitlan was celebrated in a fashion worthy of a full-scale triumph in ancient Rome, with prisoners being brought home not just for parade, but for the customary ritual sacrifice. Before tackling the Tarascans more directly, in 1478, Axayácatl finalised Montezuma Ilhuacamina's conquest of the Huaxtecs around Tuxpan on the coast of the Gulf of Mexico.

The Tarascans were formidable, a mighty military power with a considerable empire of their own to defend and one of the few peoples of Mexico able to outnumber the Aztecs. Tarascan confidence was evident in the sarcastic message they sent to the *tlatoani* on learning of his preparations for war. 'Great Lord,' Tarascan emissaries told Axayácatl, 'What has brought you hither? . . . Were you not happy in your own land? . . . Look to what you do, Lord, for you have been most ill-advised.' (Durán, Vol. 2, p. 283)

Axayácatl's first instinct was to heed the implicit warning, but his captains apparently talked him out of it and the Aztec campaign went forward. Disaster ensued. The Aztec forces were bundled into retreat by a superior foe fighting on their home ground and returned, deeply humiliated, to Tenochtitlan. This crushing defeat was never reversed and the Tarascans were still a threat on the fringes of the Aztec Empire when the Spaniards arrived.

Axayácatl died three years later, in 1481. His successor as *tlatoani* was his elder brother, Tizoc, who proved an unfortunate choice. Tizoc's inaugural campaign, against Metztitlan in the far north of the Aztec domains, was something of a fiasco by previous standards, even though Tizoc forced the enemy to retreat. The Aztec losses numbered 300, far too many for glory, and their prisoners totalled a paltry forty. The campaign ended with the Aztec commanders retiring from the field, preceded, it was said, by the fainthearted *tlatoani*.

In these humiliating circumstances, it seems fortunate that Tizoc's reign was short, no more than five years. His chief known achievement was to enlarge the Great Temple at Tenochtitlan and to create the Stone of Tizoc, a massive monument 2.65 metres in diameter, showing fifteen scenes depicting the victories of the Aztecs over various cities. Each portrays Tizoc with the vanquished leader. An Englishman, William Bullock, who saw the stone in 1822 after it had been unearthed from beneath the cathedral square of Mexico City, spent several days taking casts of the monument, which now resides in the National Museum of Anthropology (Bullock, pp. 333–42). The stone suggests that Tizoc was a more enterprising conqueror than his reputation gave out. He put down a rebellion in Toluca and may also have conquered parts of the present-day Mexican states of Guerrero and Oaxaca.

Tizoc died in 1486, reputedly murdered on the orders of the ruler of Ixtapalapa, whose motives remain unknown. As so often happened in Aztec history, superstition and the paranormal are presumed to have played their part in Tizoc's end, which was allegedly brought about after spells cast by witches induced him to bleed from the mouth.

The perceived incompetence of Tizoc and the restlessness among the Aztecs' subject peoples caused by lack of strength at the centre laid a particular burden on his successor. However, it was the Aztecs' great good luck that the chosen candidate, Ahuízotl, younger brother of Axayácatl and Tizoc, more than measured up to the great expectations that devolved upon him. As a military commander, Ahuízotl displayed formidable leadership qualities, with a brand of genius in strategy and tactics which have led some to compare him to Alexander the Great. Though a hot-tempered young man who could explode in demonic fury at the merest hint of disobedience, there was also a dark and mysterious side to his nature which made him withdrawn and contemplative, with a penchant for solitude. Consequently, Ahuízotl was regarded as a somewhat sinister figure, a reputation reinforced by the scale of human sacrifice which occurred during his reign. The first of many thousands to die at the Temple of Huitzilopochtli in Tenochtitlan were the mass of prisoners taken by Ahuízotl in his inaugural campaign against Xiquipilco, north-west of the Aztec capital, and later Chiapa and Xilotepec. In each place, the temple strongholds were stormed and the priests slaughtered, and there was so much zest for pillage that at Xilotepec, the Aztec soldiers had to be physically dragged away by their captains after Ahuízotl ordered an end to the orgy of plunder.

Ahuízotl's coronation was an occasion of the utmost luxury and splendour, deliberately designed to display the greatness of the Aztec state, its wealth, its power and its determination to inspire terror in both subjects and rivals. Considering the mastery which the Aztecs now exercised, it seems curious that they felt the need to hammer home this message. However, it was in the nature of Aztec and other Mesoamerican cultures to equate display with glory. A ruler unable or unwilling to put on a big, brash show, especially on important occasions, was diminished in the eyes of his peers and his people.

There was another reason behind the gaudy magnificence customary on the big Aztec occasion. Aztec power was not as solidly based as its vast domains made out. For instance, Xiquipilco and other towns in the area north-west of Tenochtitlan had already been conquered, but not consolidated, before Ahuízotl conquered them again. This was a frequent occurrence early on in a new reign, when subject peoples had to be shown that a change of ruler in Tenochtitlan must not be taken as a cue to rebel. In addition, Tenochtitlan still had its opponents in and around the Valley of Mexico. One invitee, the ruler of Cholula, had to be bribed to attend the coronation of Ahuízotl. Others, like the Tlaxcalans, refused outright, as did the Tarascans, who were still aglow after the humiliation they had dealt Axayácatl eight years before. This is why, the next time invitations went out from Tenochtitlan, this time to attend the inauguration of the completed Temple of Huitzilopochtli in 1487, Ahuízotl made it clear that refusal meant war. Most invitees came, to be greeted with gifts and feasts and a grandstand view of the orgy of human sacrifice which sealed the ceremony in streams of blood over the five days that it lasted.

Ahuízotl soon proceeded to reinforce these shows of power and splendour with new conquests. He began with Teloloapan, south-west of Tenochtitlan, one of the few places which had dared not to send representatives to see the temple dedicated. Blood flowed in the streets when the Aztecs answered this insult with a massive assault and a wholesale massacre of the city's inhabitants. Oztoma and Alahuiztla were next on the list, and in both places every adult was slaughtered while the young were carried off as war booty. Afterwards, the two cities were repopulated by emigrants from the Triple Alliance cities of Tenochtitlan, Texcoco and Tacuba. At around this time, in 1488, a similar fate befell the Zapotec region of Oaxaca, where the bodies of the dead were ruthlessly pillaged for valuables.

The decimation of Oztoma, and the installation there of a new population drawn from Triple Alliance cities who were therefore more likely to be loyal to Tenochtitlan, had another purpose beyond revenge. Oztoma was strategically placed close to Tarascan country. Ahuízotl was too shrewd to attempt a full-scale assault in that direction: Axayácatl's disastrous experience held him back from making a similar mistake. Instead, Oztoma was heavily fortified and added to a line of citadels which, like the Great Wall of China, was designed to deter a dangerous enemy from invading the empire.

Ahuízotl's next conquests also had Tarascan connotations. The Aztec–Tarascan border stretched across central America from the Gulf of Mexico almost to the shores of the Pacific Ocean. Aztec security therefore required Aztec control along its entire frontier and between 1491 and 1495, Ahuízotl's armies added to his empire a 240 km stretch of Pacific coastland, from Zacatula to Acapulco.

It was to prove a tragic irony, however, that with the Pacific coast campaign the Aztec Empire had nearly reached its greatest extent, while simultaneously the instrument of its future destruction was probing the offshore islands to the east. On 12 October 1492 Christopher Columbus, sailing west to reach the riches of Cathay and Cipango – China and Japan – is generally believed to have landed on the Bahamian island of Guanahani, later called San Salvador, just as Ahuízotl was putting the finishing touches to his domains. From there, Columbus went on to Cuba and Haiti, on the island later called Hispaniola, where the first European colonists arrived in 1498, shortly before Ahuízotl conquered Tehuantepec, close to the Isthmus of Panama.

By 1500 Amerigo Vespucci was discovering that America was not an outlying part of Asia, as Columbus believed, but a previously unknown – and very extensive – continent. In that year, Ahuízotl was campaigning in Soconusco, on the isthmus beyond Tehuantepec. It was his last war, and Soconusco his last imperial acquisition.

The same year, Tenochtitlan was flooded. Ostensibly, the cause of the trouble was a newly completed aqueduct. The Aztec approach to the problem displayed that characteristic mixture of faith and technology: the requisite sacrifices were made to Tlaloc, the Rain God, and divers painted blue, the colour of Tlaloc, were sent down to stop the floods by blocking off the waters at source.

Ahuízotl died two years later. He was comparatively young, in his thirties, and succumbed either to the latent effects of an injury sustained during the flood or to an infection contracted in Soconusco. Ahuízotl's successor was his nephew, Montezuma Xocoytzin, a son of Axayácatl, thirty-four years old and already politically and militarily experienced. Of the many candidates among the sons of Axayácatl and his brothers, Montezuma Xocoytzin was clearly the most outstanding. 'They

elected Montezuma with so much ease, because . . .
as well as being most valiant, he was grave and
temperate, so that people marvelled when they
heard him speak . . . and thus before becoming
king, he was feared and revered.' (Codex Ramírez,
p. 94; Clavijero, pp. 130–1; Durán, Vol. 2, p. 400)
This commanding personality is very different from
the timid, pliant *tlatoani* of both Spanish and Aztec
accounts who, in 1519, confronted the most resolute
and rapacious enemy the Aztecs would ever know.

THREE

Aztec Society

Despite the reverence inspired by the divine *tlatoani*, Aztec society was at heart a meritocracy. High office and high status could be earned, usually through feats of valour in war, and the ranks of the *tetecuhtin*, the nobility, were open to anyone able to qualify. Despite his élitism, Montezuma Ilhuacamina created a special noble class, the *quauhpilli*, or 'eagle lords', to honour valiant commoners. One passport to these heights was the capture of at least three enemies in battle, and their delivery to the priests for sacrifice. This feat, which Montezuma Xocoytzin achieved by the time he was eighteen, conferred the honoured title of Master of Cuts. Montezuma was also allowed to advertise his prowess by wearing the leather earplugs, eagle-feather headband and fringed, tufted hairstyle of the fully fledged warrior.

Of course, Montezuma and his predecessors belonged to a 'royal family' which in Aztec terms meant the ruling *calpulli*, the most prominent in a society made up of hundreds of such clans. Each *calpulli* existed as a minor state in its own right and consisted of up to 200 nuclear families: a man, his wife, their unmarried children, and the households of their married sons or brothers. The land, communally owned, was shared out for cultivation between the households. By the nature of their environment, rural *calpulli* were found in small towns or in a group of villages. Larger *calpulli* were confined mainly to the larger Aztec towns and the cities, where they occupied neighbourhoods.

Each clan had its own ruling council, selected from the heads of the households, and a *tlatoani* of its own who normally belonged to a leading family. Each *calpulli* paid group taxes to the central government and ran its own schools for girls or for young men, where military and moral training were high on the timetable. Each owed duties to the government, providing obligatory unpaid labour for agricultural, construction and other projects and performing military service. The watchwords of this carefully organised society were duty, discipline and devotion to the gods, and that applied equally to the *tlatoani* in Tenochtitlan and the lowliest member of the smallest *calpulli*.

Even so, there were clear divisions within Aztec society as a whole. Alongside or only just below the *tlatoani* were the priests, whose functions embraced not only the direction and practice of religion, but participation in war and government. The *tlatoani* himself frequently belonged to the priestly class as well as being born into the *tetecuhtin*. As a group, the *tetecuhtin* were generally ranked below the *tlatoani* and included the professional soldiers. The *macehualtin*, the class of free commoners, stood below them. There were also the *mayeques*, or serfs, who worked on the rural estates, some of which were private- and some state-owned. The unfortunates termed 'pawns' were poor Aztecs who sold themselves or members of their families in return for sustenance and housing. They were not slaves *per se*: the limit on their service made them more like indentured labourers. Nevertheless, in Aztec society there were real slaves, the *tlatoctli*, who were bought and sold at markets like any other commodity. Many of them ended their lives as human sacrifices.

There were, too, shades of difference within each class. The *tetecuhtin* who held no political office and had inherited no private estates became dependent on the *tlatoani*, while others who occupied state

43

positions and owned land were more respectably placed. Among the *macehualtin*, merchants, jewellers, goldsmiths, featherworkers and sculptors had a higher status than those with more mundane occupations. Privilege, whether earned or inherited, required higher standards of behaviour. For instance, a serious crime, such as drunkenness, incurred the death penalty when committed by a *tecuhtli*, whereas a *macehual* would be given a second chance. As punishment, though, his head would be shaved and his house knocked down. Only if he was found drunk a second time would a *macehual* be executed. At the same time, it was necessary that the *macehualtin* be seen to know their place. For instance, wearing cotton clothes was a monopoly of the higher classes. So were elaborate jewellery, beautiful plumes, perfumes, presents of roses and certain luxury foods such as cocoa. A commoner caught aping his 'betters' in any of these ways was liable to be killed for his temerity.

The *tetecuhtin* may have enjoyed the cream of what their society had to offer, including large tracts of land, but in return the Aztec state demanded service from them and particularly military service. Because of the perennial need to provide prisoners as human sacrifices, the Aztec state could not afford protracted periods of peace. Montezuma Ilhuacamina, in fact, issued a decree that war was the most important factor in Aztec life and that the *tetecuhtin* could enjoy none of their privileges unless they had war experience and better still, physical evidence of wounds sustained in battle.

The warlike nature of the tribes in the Valley of Mexico and beyond and their ongoing rivalries, together with the exigencies of empire-building and the provision of victims as part of the tribute exacted from subject peoples, usually meant that a plentiful supply of sacrifices was maintained. However, where there was a shortfall, the Aztecs would stage the ritual ceremony known as the War of the Flowers, in which a set-piece battle was organised so that each side could take prisoners and afterwards offer them to their gods.

The mentality that could accept war as normal and sacrifice as an honourable fate, willingly embraced, was forged in childhood by schooling of the most rigorous kind. In the clan *telpochcalli*, the house of youth for commoners, boys were taught humility by hard, menial work such as sweeping floors and making adobe bricks for house-building, while also learning history and religious rituals and the handling of weapons in war. For girls the training was less arduous; they were taught housecraft as a precursor to their one and only destiny in life: marriage and motherhood.

Nevertheless, disobedience or laziness by either sex was punished in the most ferocious manner. Boys or girls might be held over a fire made of chilli peppers and forced to breathe in clouds of bitter-smelling, choking smoke. The sharp spines of the maguey cactus would be driven into their flesh and afterwards they would be tied hand and foot and made to lie on wet, soggy ground for a day (Codex Mendoza, pp. 69, 74–8). As a means of inculcating obedience, all this seems tantamount to torture to the modern and especially the Western mind. To the Aztecs, however, it was a necessary precursor to adult life in which personal preferences always took second place to the needs and demands of the Aztec state and especially to the frequent incidence of warfare.

Although there was a military élite, the Eagle and Ocelot warriors from whose ranks commanders were drawn, the Aztec army was basically a citizen force whose rank-and-file had to enter service ready trained to withstand long, forced marches and gruelling living conditions. Above all, they had to know how to obey orders and wield weapons.

None of these weapons was made of metal, which in the Aztec world was largely reserved for artwork and decoration. Nevertheless, the power of these implements to kill and injure was awesome. The Aztec *tlacochtli*, or javelin, was made of cane wood with a flint or obsidian glass head. Arrows, too, were tipped with obsidian. Probably the most fearsome weapons in the Aztec armoury were the three-pronged darts with cords attached so that they could be retrieved after use. Running a close second was the *maquihuitl*, a wooden sword about 1 metre long set with two obsidian blades. The *maquihuitl* was capable of shredding flesh and, as the Spaniards later discovered, could cut the head off a horse with a single blow.

Although Montezuma Ilhuacamina had given warfare prime place in Aztec life, the great majority of Aztecs were farmers or craftsmen. Most were born into their work in life, as it was the norm to follow in a father's or mother's footsteps. Girls were introduced to home-making early on and by the time they were seven years old they knew how to use a spindle and make thread. Grinding maize and kneading it into dough, cooking, caring for babies, and weaving cloth on looms were further lessons which girls absorbed in preparation for their future domestic life and duties.

Aztec girls were expected to marry at age ten or twelve, Aztec boys in their late teens. Marriages were arranged, usually by the parents, although the young people were not forced into it since Aztec custom allowed for the fact that however good a match might look on paper, as it were, they might not be personally compatible.

A bride would be decorated for the wedding ceremony by having her face covered in yellow paste and her arms and legs covered with red feathers. The match-maker who had organised the union would carry her on his back to the house of the bridegroom's parents, where the ceremony was to take place. There, the couple perfumed each other with incense, and the marriage was made when the match-maker knotted the bridegroom's cloak to the girl's blouse (Codex Mendoza, p. 74).

Despite his comparative youth, the new husband would already be well placed to establish his own household and family, having been trained from infancy. Male babies were presented with miniature shields and arrows, the tools of the soldier, and were also given the symbols of their father's work – for a farmer's son, a digging-stick and the seed bag which was hung round the neck at planting time, or for the sons of craftsmen the characteristic tools of the featherworker, jeweller, potter, tailor, stone-mason or carpenter. Later, as the boys grew up, their fathers would introduce them to work-skills in the fields or the workshop. They would also be taught general skills, such as how to catch fish, cut canes or handle a canoe.

For the sons of farmers who lived and worked on the *chinampas*, an aptitude for boating was essential. Taking to market the maize, flowers, chillis, tomatoes, squash fruits and other produce grown on these fertile garden islands, some of which could be 92 metres long and 10 metres wide, involved paddling canoes safely along the vast network of canals. Loading and packing the produce so that the canoe would not sink on the way was a special skill in itself.

At the market-place, or *tianquiz*, a dizzying choice of vegetables as well as meats, fish and other foods and items would be on sale at stalls or shops. When the Spaniards arrived in Tenochtitlan in 1519, it had up to 300,000 inhabitants, augmented by thousands more who were willing to make long journeys on foot from the surrounding areas to attend the markets held there every five days. This was more than enough to support the vast amount of trade carried on in the capital, which was the hub of a market network extending throughout the Valley of Mexico. In the second of five lengthy reports, written on 30 October 1520, Cortés told King Charles of Spain of the variety to be found in the markets of the city he called 'Temixtitan':

This city has many squares where trading is done and markets are held continuously. There is also one square twice as big as that of Salamanca, with arcades all around, where more than 60,000 people come each day to buy and sell, and where every kind of merchandise produced in these lands is found; provisions, as well as ornaments of gold and silver, lead, brass, copper, tin, stones, shells, bones and feathers. They also sell lime, hewn and unhewn stone, adobe bricks, tiles and cut and uncut woods of various kinds. There is a street where they sell game and birds of every species found in this land: chickens, partridges, and quails, wild ducks, fly-catchers, widgeons, turtledoves, pigeons, cane birds, parrots, eagles and eagle owls, falcons, sparrow hawks and kestrels. . . .

There are streets of herbalists where all the medicinal herbs and roots found in the land are sold. There are shops like apothecaries', where they sell ready-made medicines as well as liquid ointments and plasters (Cortés, 2nd letter, pp. 103–5).

Cortés went on to list honey, wax, syrups made from maize canes, and the maguey cactus, sugar, wine, cotton, deerskins, earthenware, maize, maize bread, chicken, fish pies, salted fish, eggs, including goose eggs, and tortillas. The Aztec diet was even more extensive than this. As Cortés noted in this and his other letters to his sovereign, the menu also included chilli peppers, onions, leeks, garlic, watercress, sorrel, artichokes, cherries, plums, and *pulque*, a heady drink made from the fermented juice of the maguey.

However, nowhere in all this bustle of trade did any money change hands, since the Aztecs knew nothing of coins but traded entirely by barter and exchange. The nearest they came to money as the Spaniards understood it was in the gold dust, cacao beans and T-shaped bars of copper they used as small change. When Bernal Díaz visited the market at Tlatelolco, which was even more vast than those in Tenochtitlan, he observed how the barter system worked. In the great temple, Bernal wrote: 'there were many . . . merchants who sold gold in grains as it came from the mines. They put it in goose quills. . . . They calculated how much so many blankets or gourds of cacao were worth, or slaves, or whatever else they traded, according to the length and thickness of the quills.'

The problem with barter and exchange was, of course, the unstandardised nature of the 'currency' used. In the absence of a single unit of exchange, value was often a matter of opinion, and opinions could clash. Consequently the Aztec markets had their own courts comprising ten or twelve judges. Their task was to regulate trading, with special reference to the danger of giving short measure. As long as the market was open, officials mingled with the crowds 'observing what it sold and the measures with which it is measured'. Bernal added 'We saw one measure broken which was false.' Punishments for wrongdoing could be a great deal worse than this: anyone found guilty of stealing was flogged to death on the spot.

Needless to say, the rules about giving proper measures were extremely strict and covered a multitude of goods, including paper, paint, glue, feathers, rubber, salt, obsidian blades and mirrors, pottery, jewels, baskets, lengths of cloth, herbs and potions, or slaves. Maize and grains, for instance, were sold in measures of about 90 kg called *troje*, or about 60 kg, called *tlacopintli*. Cloth was reckoned by the length of a hand, by the *cemmitl* – the distance between outstretched arms – or by a longer measurement from the ground to the tips of the fingers when the arm was stretched above the head. However, there were some fixed 'prices' in which the 'currency' was a number of *quachtli*, or cloaks. For instance, a slave who was good at dancing was worth forty cloaks, while one without such talent merited only about thirty. A canoe cost one cloak, a gold lip-plug cost twenty-five cloaks, and a military costume with a feathered shield, sixty-four. A string of jade beads was a luxury item: it cost six hundred cloaks.

The Aztec *pochteca*, the merchants, were something of a class apart within the ranks of the *macehualtin*. They enjoyed more privileges than was usual for commoners – they had their own lawcourts – but the nature of their work meant that they also took more than the usual risks. Trading journeys could last for a year or more, and safety could never be guaranteed as the trading caravans crossed hot, thirsty deserts, dangerous mountain passes and fast-flowing rivers. Hostile tribes might attack them, or merchants could die from drinking infected water, eating bad food and sometimes from sheer exhaustion.

The rituals observed before a caravan set out reflected these dangerous possibilities. First, the stars would be consulted to ensure that the day of departure was a lucky one. Once the date was decided, the merchants, their wives and children would ceremonially wash their heads and cut their hair, and none of them would do these things again until the merchants had returned safely. Then, some time during the night, the merchants would slip silently from their homes. By the time their families woke next morning, they would be far away and out of sight, somewhere in the mountains.

FOUR

Religion, Myth and Magic

The departure of the *pochteca* under cover of darkness was tantamount to an act of courage, for the Aztecs were an intensely superstitious people. At night, they believed, ghastly demons were abroad and there were fearful visions lurking about. In his guise as the god of witches and magicians, Tezcatlipoca lay in wait round dark corners or in the shadows. He could appear as a corpse wrapped in a shroud or as a figure with no head, split open from chest to stomach. Ghosts of people who had died violent deaths awaited behind trees and rocks, and towns and cities were full of evil spirits which hovered about the streets, waiting to terrify those unwise enough to venture out.

The fear and dread implicit in such beliefs was reflected in the Aztec religion. For them, the gods were perennially angry and threatening, and the practice of their faith was an ongoing effort to fend off calamity. The greatest effort, of course, was directed towards ensuring that Huitzilopochtli, the Sun, who was thought to die each sunset, would be able to rise next morning. He was given the strength to do so through the blood of human sacrifices. This was part of a *quid pro quo* arrangement, in which the gods were repaid for sacrificing themselves in order to create the world.

According to Aztec myth, the gods had gathered at Teotihuacan, the 'metropolis of the gods' which today is about 32 km north of Mexico City, where 'they debated who would bear the burden, who would carry on his back, and become, the Sun. And when the Sun came to arise, then all . . . died that the Sun might come unto being.' (Sahagún (1950–82), Bk 3, p. 1, Bk 7, p. 4) However, the Sun, giver and sustainer of the earth and all its life, was not a permanent fixture. Like many other peoples of Mesoamerica, the Aztecs believed that the Sun was destroyed and recreated four times before the era of the Fifth Sun in which they lived. Each time, a different god became the Sun.

The first was Tezcatlipoca, who was often portrayed as a jaguar. In this first era, the earth had been peopled by giants. However, jaguars had devoured the earth and the giants, before the second rebirth under the aegis of Quetzalcoatl, the Plumed Serpent. Hurricanes had destroyed the earth of the Second Sun, and its humans, who lived on acorns, had been metamorphosed into monkeys.

The people of the Third Sun, over which Tlaloc, god of rain, presided, had been seed-eaters, and turned into dogs, turkeys and butterflies when their world was torn apart by rain and fire. Clalchiuhtlicue, the goddess of water and the wife or sister of Tlaloc, had presided over the Fourth Sun. This time, the earth had been destroyed by a great flood and its inhabitants had become fish. The Fifth Sun was created by Tonatiuh, the sun god who was associated with the eagle and with the patron deity of the Aztecs, Huitzilopochtli. Prediction decreed that this world, into which the Spaniards intruded, would be destroyed by sky monsters.

According to Aztec belief, however, the end of the world was not a random occurrence. It would arrive only at the end of one of the 52-year cycles into which time was divided. The end of each cycle was therefore a sombre event, observed with much trepidation. It was symbolised by the ceremony of 'tying up the years' and, if all went well, the making of New Fire. The last fifty-two years, represented by a bundle of fifty-two wooden rods known as *xiuhmopilli*, would be burned. Twelve days before the end of the cycle, the Aztecs would begin a fast on bread and water and no fires would be made. Pottery, utensils, and clothing would be destroyed, and the Aztecs would offer the gods blood drawn from their ears and tongues. Then came the night when Aldebaran, the brightest star in the constellation Taurus, one hundred times brighter than the Sun, reached its zenith at midnight. If the star stood still, cataclysm was imminent. If it moved on, the world was saved and another 52-year cycle would begin. When that occurred, the priests made fire, performed the usual human sacrifice, and from the blaze the sacred flames of the temple and the fire in peoples' homes would be lit. None of them were allowed to go out until the end of the new 52-year cycle.

The careful reckonings of the Aztec calendar which included the vital 52-year cycle, lay at the heart of priestly activities. Here, a multiple and several factors of the number 52 recurred, with 13 as a sacred number; the ritual calendar consisted of

260 days. There was a cycle of thirteen numbers which ran in harness with another cycle, of twenty days. The groups were controlled by thirteen gods known as Lords of the Day as well as by thirteen sacred birds and nine Lords of the Night. In addition, Aztec cosmology envisaged thirteen heavens and nine underworlds, where the majority went after death, except for warriors, human sacrifices and women who died in childbirth. They were elevated to the Sun, whereas victims of drowning or dropsy and other 'watery' diseases went to the underworlds ruled by the *tlaloques*, the rain gods.

The solar calendar of 365 days was also used for practical purposes, in agriculture or for setting the dates of the large markets, which were held every five days, the length of the solar week, and of the smaller markets which took place every four weeks. It also had a religious function, timing the ceremonies which occurred every twenty days. It was, in fact, when the solar and the ritual calendar began on the same day, once every fifty-two years, that the end of the world was feared to be imminent.

Once the continuance of the world was assured, the priests were able to return to their regular duties. 'Ordinary' priests, known as *tlamacaqui*, 'fed' the idols in the temples, tended the temple fires or burned incense in censers with long handles shaped like snakes. Priests also had charge of the sacred painted books and ran a *calmecac* school where young boys were trained for the priesthood. Discipline, and self-discipline, were ruthless, not least in the priests' daily practice of using cactus spines to draw blood from their ears, tongues, thighs and other parts of the body as an offering to the gods.

Not all priests were eligible to perform human sacrifice. This task was reserved for an élite, the *tlenamacac*. The major site in Tenochtitlan where sacrifices were performed in public was the Templo Mayor, almost a city in its own right, surrounded by walls and 25 hectares in extent in the centre of the city. A sacrifice, *ixiptla*, or 'god's image', would be ceremonially bathed in advance to wash out all impurities and clothed in the robes and distinguishing badges of the god for whose sake he was to die. The *ixiptla* then had to climb one of two steep stairways leading to the summit, where he would be spreadeagled on the altar with four priests holding down his arms and legs and another holding his head. Using a special obsidian-bladed knife, the *tlenamacac* would cut the chest open with one swift movement, rip out the heart and hold it up as an offering to the Sun.

Great honour accrued to an *ixiptla*, who was seen as emulating the self-sacrifice by which the gods had created the Sun, and he himself became a deity at death. There was, too, a special lustre in becoming an *ixiptla* to Tezcatlipoca. His festival required a young man of sixteen or seventeen who, for a year, was garbed in gold and fine cotton, garlanded with flowers and had his every need fulfilled by eight special attendants before mounting the steps to die.

Needless to say, the Spaniards regarded human sacrifice as an abomination, all the more so since, according to Cortés, 'priests dress in black and never comb their hair from the time they enter the priesthood until they leave' (Cortés, 2nd letter, p. 105). Consequently, the Spanish accounts has depicted priests as figures of horror, their faces painted black, their bodies disfigured from driving maguey spines into their flesh and with unwashed, uncombed hair and clothes matted by the blood they spilled in such profusion.

Another priestly role, in astrology, had considerable relevance for the Aztecs. They believed not only in all kinds of spirits, but in magic, witchcraft and sorcery as well. Aztec reliance on portents was also a facet of the *tlatoani*'s role. He was supposed to observe the sky three times a day, at sunrise, sunset and midnight, and to deduce future events from cosmic activity such as the position of the planets, the incidence of shooting stars or comets, and the appearance and colour of clouds. Likewise, the wind in the trees or birds in flight had astrological significance, among the many different signs denoting good luck or the bad luck which the Aztecs made maximum efforts to avoid.

No Aztec would dream of doing anything – getting married, going on a journey, naming a child, constructing a building – until the astrologer-priests had consulted the ritual calendar and pronounced the time as favourable. This was normal in a society where everyday life was thought to be full of potentially dangerous situations. Sickness, suffering or death were foretold by the cry of a screech owl, a skunk or a rabbit in the house or the creak of roof beams. If a woman died in childbirth and became a *cuiapipiltin*, there was a risk that a sorcerer with black magic in mind might chop off and steal her forearm which was supposed to have sinister powers. The *cuiapipiltin* were reputed to haunt crossroads, and anyone unlucky enough to see one there would, the Aztecs believed, be struck by paralysis. Disease in general was believed to be a punishment from the gods, each of whom presided over certain illnesses. The rain god, Tlaloc, for instance, inflicted dropsy, gout, leprosy, swellings and ulcers by sending freezing winds from *Tlaloque*, where the mountain gods lived. The Lord Spring or the Flayed Lord, Xipe Totec, caused skin diseases and eye infections.

This was why the Aztecs frequently wore amulets to protect themselves against the anger of the gods, but if that failed and illness struck then the *tlacatecolotl*, or sorcerer-healer, would be called in. A bundle of rods would be thrown to the ground and the pattern they made examined so that the *tlacatecolotl* could locate the source of the illness. After that, treatment would consist of drugs taken from plants, such as *peyotl* made from cactus buds, or *oloiuhqui* made from the seeds of the convulvulus flower. Both these drugs were hallucinogens, enabling patients to have visions and recount the strange hallucinations they were experiencing.

These hallucinations, in their turn, might reveal the reason for the illness afflicting them.

However, medical treatments were not left entirely to the *tlacatecolotl*. The more scientific Aztec physicians, or *tlamatini*, were well aware that the damp, cold climate of the Valley of Mexico rather than the activities of evil spirits or angry gods was responsible for rheumatism, coughs, chills and other similar complaints. For these, they recommended steam-baths and also prescribed herbal drinks to purge the body and herbal ointments and a good diet for those suffering from blotches or spots. They used valerian as a stimulant, mint to relieve congested chests, and honey drinks or maguey cactus syrup for sore throats. Massage was prescribed to ease sprains, stiff necks and inflamed throats, and the *tlamatini* also knew how to set broken bones, sew up wounds with hair and lance boils or cysts.

The manifest superstitions of Aztec society naturally lent heavily on omens and portents, especially frightening ones. Belief in such portents went right to the top – a series of alarming prodigies turned Montezuma Xocoytzin, the *tlatoani* himself, from the dignified, commanding figure elected in 1502 into a man full of foreboding at the calamities which, he was convinced, were soon to overtake him.

SOME AZTEC GODS

Chalchiuhtlicue: 'The Jade Skirted One', goddess of water.

Coatlicue: 'The Serpent-Skirted One', earth goddess and mother of Huitzilopochtli.

Huitzilopochtli: 'Humming Bird of the South', the patron god of the Aztecs.

Miclantecuhtli: 'Lord of the Place of the Dead'. Always pictured as a skeleton, Miclantecuhtli ruled the underworld.

Quetzalcoatl: 'The Plumed Serpent', priest-ruler of the Toltecs, god of the planet Venus, god of the evening star (as Tlahuizcalpantecuhtli), and god of wind (as Ehécatl).

Tezcatlipoca: 'Smoking Mirror', god of the night sky and patron god of sorcerers and magicians; often depicted as a jaguar and identified with the Great Bear constellation.

Tlaloc: Possibly an earth-god; Aztec god of rain.

Tonatiu: 'He goes forth shining', the sun god; Huitzilopochtli was one of his aspects.

Xipe Totec: 'The Flayed Lord', god of vegetation, agriculture and the spring; patron of jewellers and goldsmiths; also called the Red Tezcatlipoca.

See Vaillant, *Aztecs of Mexico*, table 7, pp. 187–90; table 10, p. 197; table 12, p. 199.

See Burland, *The Gods of Mexico*, pp. ix–xi.

FIVE

Conquest

Montezuma Xoyoctzin was a martinet, or so he appeared in the first years of his reign. Once elected, he moved quickly to impose his will, and his élitist ideas, on his subjects. He cleaned out the ranks of the nobility, dismissing commoners of low birth who, in his view, degraded government and court circles by their humble lineage. Only those of royal or legitimate noble blood would henceforth be allowed to hold high or influential positions. Montezuma even went so far as to purify the Nahuatl language so that his commands, when promulgated, would not be sullied by low language.

In this and much else, Montezuma seems to have believed that he ruled by divine right. This clear shift towards absolute monarchy was a break with the more liberal royal traditions of Mexico and the prevailing concept of the *tlatoani* who, even taking his divinity into account, was seen as first among equals within a ruling team. Montezuma, however, was not interested in such precedents. Rather, he aimed to put the powerful groups in his realm – the nobility, the merchants, the military – firmly under his control and impose his own strict standards on them.

When Montezuma Xoyoctzin became *tlatoani*, the Aztec Empire was close to its greatest feasible extent, barring certain enclaves, such as Tlaxcala, Metztitlan or the Pacific coast principality of Tototepec, which remained stubbornly out of reach. However, there were several territories already conquered but not entirely pacified so that Montezuma's wars, which he led in person, were more in the nature of consolidations.

The more measured nature of Montezuma's campaigns meant that the Aztecs were on a war footing for far longer than was usual in a new reign: hostilities occupied much of Montezuma's first twelve years. During that time, however, the inflexible, somewhat despotic will of the *tlatoani* was gradually sapped by several inauspicious happenings which, as it later transpired, coincided with increasing Spanish presence in the Gulf of Mexico.

The Aztecs later interviewed by Fray Bernardino de Sahagún read these signs with hindsight, but the coincidences were significant: 'Even before the Spaniards landed . . . omens foretold their coming. . . . First, every night there arose a sign like a tongue of fire, like a flame. . . . All night, off to the east, it looked as if day had dawned. This went on for a year. . . . Next, quite of its own accord, at Itepeyoc, at Tlacateccan, Huitzilopochtli's temple burst into flame. No man's hand could have set it; it burned of itself. . . . Then lightning struck the straw roof of Tzonmulco, the temple of the old fire god Xiuhtectli. This happened not during a storm, but a mere sprinkle with just a summer flash, not even a thunderclap. Hence, it was a sign of evil.' (Sahagún (1978), Vol. 12)

As time went on, the portents proliferated – a three-headed comet hurtling from west to east, the waters of Lake Texcoco boiling up on a windless day. The seventh of eight ominous signs was the most frightening of all. Some fishermen snared a brown crane whose features were so strange that they took it to Montezuma. 'Montezuma peered, to see the heavens . . . the stars, the constellation. He was first startled and then terrified as he saw, a little beyond, what looked like fighting men massed, like conquerors in war array, riding the backs of deer.' (Sahagún (1978), Vol. 12)

Some of these and other similar occurrences can be dated. The comet appeared in 1509. In 1512 there were three earthquakes. The fire at the temple occurred soon afterwards, and next, the waters of Lake Texcoco boiled up and swamped shoreline houses on a perfectly calm day. Together with a drought in 1504, a famine in 1505 and in 1507, a plague of rodents, an eclipse of the Sun and another earthquake, this parade of evil augury so unnerved Montezuma that in 1517, when a Spanish expedition landed in mainland Mexico, he reacted not as a proud ruler outraged that strangers should dare to intrude on his realm, but as a man desperate to mollify them and, he hoped, make them go away.

By this time, the Spaniards had been exploring the eastern coasts of the American continent for many years and had seen the northern coast of South America, the stretch from Honduras to Panama and the east coast of the Yucatán peninsula of Mexico, all of them between 1499 and 1506. In 1509 the Spaniards occupied Jamaica and two years later founded a colony on the island of Cuba. It was from this base that the first explorations of mainland Mexico took place. The galleons of an expedition of 1517, headed by Fernandez de Cordoba, were reported to Montezuma as a huge mountain which had been sighted moving over the sea. Cordoba landed in the area of Campeche, but was driven off with heavy losses by the inhabitants. Undeterred, the Spaniards made a second attempt the following year. Juan de Grijalva sailed from Cuba on 1 May 1518 and this time the Spaniards made friendly contact with the natives on the island of Cozumel, off the Yucatán peninsula. From them, they learned of Culhua and 'Mexico', meaning Tenochtitlan, somewhere in the interior. Already, while sailing north as far as the River Pánuco, they had glimpsed far-off volcanoes topped with snow, a sure sign that they had come upon a vast new land.

Before long, the Aztec tax-collectors who controlled the area came to view the visitors for themselves. According to Hernando Alvarez Tezozómoc, they behaved as if the Spaniards were gods and informed Montezuma of them. Montezuma's reaction was to forbid his council to reveal anything about this development.

Down on the coast, Grijalva had decided to found a settlement and sent to Cuba and its governor, Diego de Velazquez, for help and fresh supplies. The message was taken by Pedro de Alvarado, who arrived in Cuba with gold jewellery which had been bartered with the natives. The Spaniards' reaction to this treasure was ecstatic. 'With Diego Velazquez,' wrote Bernal Díaz, who had taken part in both the Cordoba and Grijalva expeditions, 'were many men from the city and other parts of the island. When the King's officers had taken the royal fifth which is due to His Majesty, everyone was astonished at the riches of the lands we had discovered.'

With this, a larger and more ambitious third expedition gathered, this time intent on penetrating further inland and discovering the source of this phenomenal wealth. Led by Hernán Cortés, 32 crossbowmen, 13 arquebusiers, 463 other soldiers equipped with bronze cannon, 100 sailors and 16 horses sailed from Cuba on 10 February 1519 and landed at Tabasco, in south-east Mexico on 12 March. At this, Sahagún's informants recounted, 'the stewards again sped to inform Montezuma. And Montezuma acted; for he thought, as everyone else did, that it surely was Quetzalcoatl who had returned, as he had said he would.' (Sahagún (1978), Vol. 12)

A splendid display of gifts was prepared and transported down to the coast. They included four complete sets of divine array as traditionally worn by Quetzalcoatl, Tlaloc and Tezcatlipoca. With these and other magnificent presents, Montezuma hoped to bribe the Spaniards to return whence they had come and leave him alone. What he did not realise was that the gold, jadite, feathers, turquoise and other treasure would have completely the opposite effect. When, inevitably, Montezuma's blandishments failed, he resorted to his sorcerers and magicians – 'all the doers of evil he could gather' – and commanded them to get rid of the visitors by spells and incantations. When that failed, too, Montezuma at last realised that sombre prophecies made four or five years earlier by Nezahualpilli, ruler of Texcoco, son of Nezahualcóyotl and a much respected seer in Mexico, were going to come true. Montezuma wept. He was now terrified.

However, Cortés was in no hurry. His situation and that of his men was one of great potential peril. Here they were, a small band of strangers, in an unknown, uncharted land, vastly outnumbered yet aiming to reach an empire in the mountains where they would be totally isolated and well beyond the reach of aid. Cortés therefore concentrated first on exploring the coastal area, allying himself with the local Totonacs – and offering to liberate them from the hated burden of Aztec rule and tribute – and establishing a base on the coast at Veracruz.

When he finally set out for Tenochtitlan, together with an army of Totonacs, Cortés did not head directly for the capital, but instead came by way of Tlaxcala in order to swell the ranks of his forces with auxiliaries. Though the Tlaxcalans at first resisted the intruders, they finally joined the Spaniards after Cortés had gratified them by attacking and decimating the forces of their great enemy, Cholula. Thus, when Cortés marched into Tenochtitlan he came with a large and impressive array of manpower.

He also came with an advantage not given to either Cordoba or Grijalva: two interpreters. One was a Spaniard, Gerónimo de Aguilar, who had been shipwrecked on Cozumel some years earlier and had learned to speak Nahuatl. The other was a woman of noble birth, Malintzin. She had been sold into slavery and was given as a gift to Cortés by the people of Potonchan on the coast of the Gulf of

Mexico. Malintzin later became one of Cortés' many mistresses, but her knowledge of Nahuatl and Mayan, combined with Aguilar's Nahuatl and Spanish, enabled the Spaniards to communicate with the Aztecs.

As the Spaniards approached, Montezuma Xoycotzin came out along the road to Tenochtitlan to greet them in the full panoply of regal splendour. 'Montezuma descended from his litter,' wrote Bernal Díaz del Castillo 'and . . . great caciques [lords] supported him beneath a marvellously rich canopy of green feathers, decorated with gold work, silver [and] pearls. . . . It was a marvellous sight. The great Montezuma was magnificently clad . . . and wore sandals . . . the soles of which were of gold and the upper parts ornamented with precious stones. . . . Many more lords . . . walked before the great Montezuma, sweeping the ground on which he was to tread and laying down cloaks so that his feet should not touch the earth. Not one of these [lords] dared to look him in the face'.

Cortés and Montezuma exchanged gifts, but when the Spaniard moved to place a necklace of pearls, diamonds and glass jewels about the *tlatoani*'s neck, the *tetecuhtin* intervened, indicating that he was not to be touched. Cortés, as consummate a diplomat as he was a commander, knew better than to flout local custom. All the same, despite the fulsome greetings he uttered in a lengthy speech, which Montezuma matched, he had no intention of relying on displays of goodwill and hospitality to safeguard his position. Once settled in the magnificent apartments set aside for them in the royal palace in Tenochtitlan, Cortés took Montezuma hostage, intending in this way to paralyse the Aztec state by cutting off its head, as it were, and exercising control through the *tlatoani*.

Initially, the tactic was extremely effective. Montezuma was persuaded to disgorge vast amounts of gold and treasure and, at Cortés' prompting, ordered his nobles to swear alliegance to the Spanish crown. Montezuma even agreed that a shrine to the Virgin Mary be placed at the great temple pyramid in Tenochtitlan. At this stage, it must have looked as if Cortés was going to achieve a virtually bloodless takeover. However, his plans were dislocated when his jealous enemy, Diego de Velazquez, governor of Cuba, who had tried but failed to prevent him from sailing for Mexico ten months earlier, sent his crony Panfilo de Narvaez to put a stop to Cortés' empire-building activities.

Narvaez landed at Veracruz in May 1520, but his challenge was speedily ended by Cortés with a surprise guerilla-style attack. Nevertheless, this emergency had taken the Spanish commander away from Tenochtitlan and while he was absent, an even greater crisis developed in the Aztec capital. Pedro de Alvarado, the hothead whom Cortés had left in charge, attacked the Aztecs while they were celebrating a religious festival and a frightful massacre took place at the great temple. The Aztec warriors, enraged, drove the Spaniards back into the palace and there put them under siege. As a precaution, Alvarado put Montezuma in irons. When Cortés returned after seven weeks away, he found seven of his men dead, many wounded and all the survivors starving. The palace courtyard testified to the fury of the combat. It was littered with Aztec bodies and awash with blood.

Now, at long last, the Aztecs realised the ungodly nature of their visitors, and on 25 June 1520, five days after Cortés' return, they fell on the Spaniards with such savage force that within a short time they faced annihilation. In an attempt to defuse the situation, Cortés then brought out the hapless Montezuma to mediate with his subjects. It was useless: angry voices in the crowd accused him of cowardice and treachery, and according to Bernal Díaz del Castillo, 'a sudden shower of stones and darts descended. . . . Montezuma was hit by three stones, one on the head, one on the arm and one on the leg, and though they begged him to have his wounds dressed and eat some food . . . he refused.'

Four days later Montezuma died, but not as *tlatoani*: the ruling council had voted to depose him and in his place elected his brother, Quitláhuac. Though Bernal Díaz relates how Cortés and his captains wept for Montezuma, the Aztec account of this sombre event suggests a much more brutal reaction and coloured the suspicion that the Spaniards had murdered the former *tlatoani*: 'It was after another four days that the Spaniards threw the dead bodies of Montezuma and Itzquauhtzin [Montezuma's nephew] out of the palace. . . . As soon as they were recognised, men quickly took up Montezuma's body and carried it to Copulco, placed it on a pile of wood and fired it. . . . As he burned, onlookers berated him: their goodwill had given way to fury. "This blockhead" they said "terrorised the world. He kept the world in dread, in fear. . . ." And they would groan, cry out and shake disapproving heads.' (Sahagún (1978), Vol. 12)

Cortés now had no option but to get out of Tenochtitlan. The cost was enormous: the Spaniards suffered horrific losses as they struggled out of the city across one of its causeways on the night of 30 June. Two-thirds of them were killed or captured and sacrificed by the priests on what came to be known as *Noche Triste*, the Night of Sorrows. All the artillery was lost, together with most of the treasure and several horses. All the survivors, including Cortés, were wounded, many seriously. Nevertheless, the iron-willed Cortés rallied them and marched them the 96 km to the territory of his allies, the Tlaxcalans. Incredible as it may seem, the Spaniards overcame a vast horde of Aztecs who attempted to ambush them on the way, on the plain of Otumba on 7 July.

In Tlaxcala, Cortés immediately set about planning his return to Tenochtitlan. To this end, he first neutralised the pro-Aztec towns on and around Lake Texcoco and its approaches, in order to isolate the Aztecs and safeguard the route to Tlaxcala from Veracruz. Along this route fresh troops soon arrived from the Spanish colonies on Cuba, Jamaica and

Hispaniola, together with arms, supplies and horses. Cortés also persuaded some 100,000 tributaries of the Aztecs to exercise their hatred for their masters by joining his own small force, which ultimately numbered 700 soldiers, 86 cavalry, 118 arquebusiers and crossbowmen and 15 guns. In addition, Cortés had thirteen brigantines built on Lake Texcoco with total crews numbering 300 men. Their purpose was to bombard Tenochtitlan.

Meanwhile, in the capital, the Spaniards had left behind an insidious weapon: smallpox. 'The illness was so dreadful that no one could walk or move. . . . The sick were so utterly helpless that they could only lie on the beds like corpses. . . . A great many died from this plague and many others died of hunger. They could not get up to search for food and everyone else was too sick to care for them, so they starved to death in their beds.' (Sahagún (1978), Vol. 12)

Cortés moved on the Aztec capital on 28 April 1521. As he soon discovered, it was to be a fight to the death, for despite the ravages of smallpox, the Aztec defence was ferocious. After failing to take his objective by frontal assault along the three causeways, Cortés put the city under a siege which lasted over fifteen weeks. As the brigantines and other artillery pounded the city, Cortés' forces cut off the food and water supplies, and the Aztecs were forced to search among the rubble and the wrecked *chinampas* for whatever they could find – lizards, small birds, grass, weeds. Gradually, the Spaniards and their allies pushed further and further into the city. They were met by a deluge of arrows, stones and other missiles. Men, women and even children who had nothing to fight with leapt out at the Spaniards and attacked them with their bare hands.

Day and night, the temple gongs and drums boomed and the conch-shells blared as the Aztecs sacrificed to the gods and begged them to come to their aid. They begged in vain. The Spaniards eventually fought their way into the main square where, to their horror they found the heads of Spanish prisoners stuck on a row of poles. Several times, the Spaniards demanded that the Aztecs surrender. The Aztecs refused, maintaining that they would rather fight on until all of them were dead. A crowd of starving women and children came forward to give themselves up, but they were seized by Cortés' native allies and pushed into the lake. Some 15,000 were killed, most of them by drowning. What was more, these allies, delighted that at last they could have their revenge on the hated Aztecs, ran wild inside the city, slaughtering, devastating and burning.

By this time, the streets and canals of Tenochtitlan were full of rubble from the wrecked houses and temples and the dead were heaped in the streets. High above the city, there hung a huge, choking cloud of smoke from the Spaniards' guns. The Aztec commanders knew the end when they saw it. The *tlatoani* Quitláhuac had died of smallpox and his successor, his nephew Quahtemoc, a son of Ahuízotl, met with other leaders 'to decide among themselves how to offer tribute and submission to the Spaniards. After a while, Quahtemoc left in a boat with two companions, his personal page Yaztachimal and the brave warrior Tepotzitoloc. . . . The people wept as they saw him go: "Already noble young Quahtemoc is leaving to surrender himself to the gods, the Spaniards." They captured him and disembarked him . . . then they escorted him to the rooftop to present him to Cortés, who first stroked Quahtemoc with his hand then had him sit by him.' (Sahagún (1978), Vol. 12) Quahtemoc survived for about four years in Spanish captivity before he was hanged in 1525, ostensibly for plotting to kill Cortés and some of his captains. The capture of the last Aztec tlatoani signalled the end of the struggle, and soon afterwards the Spaniards fired a volley from their guns, proclaiming their victory.

So, on 13 August 1521, Tenochtitlan finally fell into Spanish hands. Some 240,000 Aztecs, three-quarters of the population, had been killed or had died of disease or starvation, and where formerly a great and beautiful metropolis had stood, nothing was left but smoking, bloodstained ruin.

Postscript

The defeat of the Aztecs was the most thorough decimation of an enemy in war that the Valley of Mexico had ever seen. However, if total war as the Spaniards waged it was alien to the Aztecs, so was its aftermath. The Aztecs may have been conquerors, but they were not generally occupiers and had little or no concept of an imperial bureaucracy. Their purpose was to win, subdue, arrange tribute and go home. It was therefore natural that the Aztecs should expect the Spaniards to do much the same. They could not have been more mistaken. The Spaniards' purpose was to colonise, exploit and impose their foreign rule and foreign ways.

Aztec Mexico was only the first of many Spanish conquests in central and North America. Eventually, the viceroyalty of New Spain also covered El Salvador, Guatemala, Honduras, California, south-west USA and Florida. Over all this vast area, the Aztecs and other native Americans found themselves sucked into a world of new and disturbing experiences. Thousands of immigrants crossed the Atlantic to settle on their lands. Their new overlord, the viceroy, ruled in the name of and under the direction of the king in distant Spain. A new capital, Mexico City, was built over the ruins of Tenochtitlan together with many other Spanish towns likewise founded on Aztec sites. Here, typically, the temples which had been the focus of the Aztec faith were torn down and churches built in their place.

The *encomiendas* established in the countryside were perhaps more familiar. In these Spanish estates the Aztecs were required to donate their labour and pay tribute, usually in the form of food and other domestic requirements, along lines not all that different from their own *calpulli* system. The *encomenderos*, for their part, were supposed to protect the Aztecs in their charge and oversee their conversion to Christianity. The system was, nevertheless, greatly weighted in the Spaniards' favour, giving them enormous potential for personal power and freedom.

In these circumstances the exploitation of native labour was inevitable, both on the land and in the silver mines, which under the Spaniards were worked as never before. This situation created such alarm in Spain that commissioners were specially sent out to curb *encomendero* excesses. The priests, whose main task was to effect conversions, were forced to double as protectors of their new flocks from *encomendero* demands. The most vociferous of these churchmen was undoubtedly Bartolomé de Las Casas, the Dominican who became Bishop of Chiápas in 1545 and was known as the 'Apostle of the Indies' for his championship of the native cause. Las Casas demonised the Spanish settlers, lashing them in the most vitriolic terms for their cruelty towards the natives.

The Aztecs themselves also made problems for the priests. Most conversions were superficial: a case of obeying orders rather than feeling spiritually drawn to seek salvation through Christ. What is more, in the undertow of the new imposed faith, Aztec devotion to their own gods survived. So did human sacrifice, even if the practice, banned by the Spaniards, had now become clandestine.

Even worse was the biological effect of the Spanish presence. The Aztecs died in droves from European diseases to which they had no resistance, a form of collateral slaughter later repeated all over Spanish America. In New Spain, measles, smallpox and mumps proved to be mass killers. An epidemic of typhus which started in 1545 and raged for three years left only 40 per cent of Aztecs unscathed. Overall, by 1570 the native population had been reduced from over 1.5 million to only 325,000. In addition, the pure-blood element among those descended from these survivors largely disappeared as the conquerors took Aztec wives and mistresses. In time, they peopled New Spain with a majority of half-breed *mestizos* who today account for 60 per cent of Mexicans.

The Aztec language, Nahuatl, however, survived though it became subordinate to Spanish, and today has 1.25 million speakers. So did Aztec diet and cuisine, Aztec markets and, in rural areas, Aztec housebuilding methods. In modern Mexico, there is a legacy of pride in the Aztec civilisation and Mexican governments actively promote archaeological investigation into the Aztec past.

Yet in the longer historical view, these are only remnants of a once-great empire and a brilliant, if bloodstained, civilisation. The Aztecs themselves are gone, cut short at the height of their power by a foe much more advanced where it mattered most. For the Aztecs encountered the Spaniards at a peak of their military prowess and imperial vigour, and, in the brutal, yet brilliant, *conquistadores*, encountered them in their most implacable guise.

Glossary

Anahuac	Valley of Mexico
Aztec	Name taken from the Aztecs' ancestral homeland of Aztlan ('Place of the White Heron'). An Azteclatl, or Aztec, was a person from Aztlan
Calmecac	Schools for the children of the *tetecuhtin* (Aztec nobility) and for some *macehualtin* (commoners)
Calpulli	Aztec clan
Chinampa	Floating garden island or small field built up on swamp land for cultivation
Codex, Codices	Aztec sacred or historical books painted in pictograms, e.g. Codex Mendoza
Macehual	A commoner (singular of *macehaultin*)
Mexica	Alternative name for Aztec, i.e. followers of Mexi (Aztec patron god Huitzilopochtli)
Montezuma	Aztec 'Great Speaker', also known as Moctezuma, Mocteçuçuma, Motecuhzoma or Mohtecuzomatzin (i.e. *Moh*, reverential term; *tecuhtli*, lord; *zoma*, brave; *tzin*, prince or noble)
Nahua	Alternative name for Aztec (from Nahuatl)
Nahuatl	Mesoamerican language spoken by Aztecs; transliterated phonetically by Spanish

93

	scribes, since the Aztecs had no alphabetical writing
Pochteca	Merchants (singular *pochtecatl*)
Tecuhtli	A noble (singular of *tetecuhtin*)
Tenochca	Alternative name for Aztec
Tlatoani	Aztec Great Speaker

Further Reading

PRIMARY SOURCES

(Anales de Tlatelolco): *Unos Anales de la Nación Mexicana*, Heinrich Berlin (ed.), in *Fuentes para la Historia*, No. 2 (Antigua Libreria Robredo, Mexico City, 1948)

Berdan, Frances F. and Anawalt, Patricia R. (eds): *Codex Mendoza: The Essential Codex Mendoza* (University of California Press, Berkeley, CA, 1997)

Chimalpain, Domingo Francisco de San Anton Muñon Cuauhtlehuantzin: *Relaciones Originales de Chalco-Amaquemecan* (1606–31), translated by Silvia Rendon (Fondo de Cultura Económica, Mexico City, 1964)

Codex Boturini (Tira de la Peregrinación) (Libréria Anticuaria, Mexico City, 1944)

Codex Mendoza (*c.* 1541/2): *Aztec Manuscript: Commentaries by Kurt Ross* (Miller Graphics, London, 1978)

Codex Ramírez (Editorial Leyenda, Mexico City, 1944)

Cortés, Hernán: *Letters from Mexico (1519–26)* (Oxford University Press, Oxford, 1972)

Díaz del Castillo, Bernal: *The Conquest of New Spain*, translated by J.M. Cohen (Penguin Classic, London, 1963)

Durán, Fray Diego (1581): *Book of the Gods and Rites and the Ancient Calendar* (University of Oklahoma Press, Tulsa, 1971)

Durán, Fray Diego (1581): *Historia de Las Indias de Nueva España e Islas de la Tierra Firme*, 2 volumes (Editorial Porrúa, Mexico City, 1967)

Ixlilxóchitl, Fernando de Alva (of Texcoco): *Obras Históricas*, 2 volumes (Editorial Nacional, Mexico City, 1952)

Las Casas, Bartolomé de (*c.* 1570): *Tratados* (Fondo de Cultural Económica, Mexico City/Buenos Aires, 1965)

León-Portilla, Miguel: *The Broken Spears: The Aztec Account of the Conquest of Mexico* (Beacon Press, Boston, 1962)

Muñoz Camargo, Diego: *Historia de Tlaxcala* (Publicaciones del Ateneo de Ciencias y Artes de Mexico, Mexico City, 1947)

Sahagún, Fray Bernardino de: *Codex Florentino: Historia General de Las Cosas de la Nueva España* (*General History of the Things of New Spain*), *The War of Conquest: How it was waged here in Mexico City* (orig. 1575–7), modern translation by Arthur J.O. Anderson and Charles E. Dibble of Book 12 (of 12 original books) (University of Utah Press, Salt Lake City, 1978)

Sahagún, Fray Bernardino de: *Codex Florentino: Historia General de Las Casas de la Nueva España* (*General History of the Things of New Spain*) (orig., 1575–7), translated by Arthur J.O. Anderson and Charles E. Dibble. Complete text. Subjects: Aztecs, Indians of Mexico, Antiquities of Mexico, History, Conquest, 1519–1540, Natural History (University of Utah Press, Salt Lake City, 1950–82)

Tezozómoc, Fernando Alvarez (1609): *Crónica Mexicayotl* (Editorial Leyenda, Mexico City, 1944)

Torquemada, Fray Juan de: *Monarquía Indiana*, 3 volumes (1592–1613) (Editorial Chavez Hayhoe, Mexico City, 1943–4)

Zorita, Alonso de: *Life and Labour in Ancient Mexico (1566–1570)*, translated by Benjamin Keen (Rutgers University Press, New Brunswick, NJ, 1963)

MODERN BOOKS

Berdan, Frances: *The Aztecs of Central Mexico: An Imperial Society* (Holt, Rinehart & Winston, New York, 1984)

Berdan, Frances F., Blanton, Richard E., Boome, Elizabeth H., Hodge, Mary G., Smith, Michael E. and Umberger, Emily: *Aztec Imperial Strategies*, essays on the economic and political geography of the Aztec Empire (Dumbarton Oaks Research Library & Collection, Washington DC, 1996)

Bernal, Ignacio and Eckholm, Gordon (eds): *Archaeology of Northern Mesoamerica, Part 1.* Article: 'Religion in Prehispanic Central Mexico' by H.B. Nicholson. *Handbook of Middle American Indians*, vol. 10 (University of Texas Press, Austin, 1971)

Boone, Elizabeth H. (ed.): *The Aztec Templo Mayor* (Dumbarton Oaks, Washington, DC, 1987)

Brundage, Burr C.: *The Jade Steps: A Ritual Life of the Aztecs* (University of Utah Press, Salt Lake City, 1985)

Burland C.A. (Cottie) with Werner Forman: *Gods and Fate in Ancient Mexico* (Panorama Editorial, Mexico City, 1980)

——: *Montezuma, Lord of the Aztecs* (Weidenfeld & Nicolson, London, 1972)

——: *The Gods of Mexico* (Eyre & Spottiswoode, 1967)

Bullock, William: *Six Months' Residence and Travel in Mexico* (John Murray, London, 1824)

Carrasco, David: *Quetzalcoatl and the Irony of Empire: Myths and Prophecies in the Aztec Tradition* (University of Chicago Press, Chicago, 1992)

Clavijero, Francisco Xavier: *Historia Antigua de Mexico* (Editorial Porrúa, Mexico City, 1964)

Clendinnen, Inga: *Aztecs* (Cambridge University Press, Cambridge, 1992)

Davies, Nigel: *The Aztecs* (Abacus, London, 1977)

——: *The Toltecs until the Fall of Tula* (University of Oklahoma Press, Tulsa, 1977)

——: *The Toltec Heritage: From the Fall of Tula to the Rise of Tenochtitlan* (University of Oklahoma Press, Tulsa, 1980)

——: *The Aztec Empire: The Toltec Resurgence* (University of Oklahoma Press, Tulsa, 1987)

Fagan, Brian: *The Aztecs* (Freeman, New York, 1984)

Gibson, Charles: *The Aztecs under Spanish Rule: History of the Indians of the Valley Mexico, 1519–1810* (Stanford University Press, 1964)

Gruzinski, Serge: *The Aztecs: Rise and Fall of an Empire*, English translation (Thames & Hudson, London, 1992)

Hassig, Ross: *Aztec Warfare: Imperial Expansion and Political Control* (University of Oklahoma Press, Tulsa, 1988)

Johnson, William Weber: *Cortés* (Hutchinson, London, 1977)

Kellogg, Susan: *Law and the Transformation of Aztec Culture 1500–1700* (University of Oklahoma Press, Tulsa, 1995)

León-Portilla, Miguel: *Aztec Thought and Culture* (University of Oklahoma Press, Tulsa, 1963)

Lockhart, James: *The Nahuas After the Conquest: A Social and Cultural History of the Indians of Central Mexico, 16th through 18th Centuries* (Stanford University Press, Stanford, CA, 1992)

Madariaga, Salvador de: *Hernán Cortés, Conqueror of Mexico* (Hodder & Stoughton, London, 1942)

Matos Moctezuma, Eduardo: *The Great Temple of the Aztecs* (Thames & Hudson, London, 1988)

Ortiz de Montellano, Bernard R.: *Aztec Medicine, Health and*

Nutrition (Rutgers University Press, New Brunswick, NJ, 1990)

Pasztory, Esther: *Aztec Art* (Harry N. Abrams, New York, 1983)

Prescott, William: *History of the Conquest of Mexico* (Random House, New York, 1843, numerous subsequent editions)

Smith, Michael E.: *The Aztecs (The Peoples of America)* (Blackwell Publishers, Oxford, 1996)

Soustelle, Jacques: *Daily Life of the Aztecs on the Eve of the Spanish Conquest* (Stanford University Press, Stanford, CA, 1961)

Taube, Karl: *Aztec and Maya Myths* (University of Texas Press, Austin, 1993)

Townsend, Richard F.: *The Aztecs* (Thames & Hudson, London, 1992)

Vaillant, George: *Aztecs of Mexico* (Pelican Books, 1962, originally published by Doubleday & Co., London, 1944)

Veytia, Mariano: *Historia Antigua de Mexico*, 2 volumes (Editorial Leyenda, Mexico City, 1944)

GENERAL

There are numerous general books on Aztec history, culture, customs, religion and other aspects. Among the most wide-ranging is Vaillant (1944), though scholarship and archaeology over the nearly sixty years since it was written have outdated some of the author's conclusions. Others which build up a comprehensive picture of Aztec civilisation as a whole are Soustelle (1961), Fagan (1984), Townsend (1992) and Clendinnen (1992). Davies (1977) is generous with descriptions of the elections and coronations of Aztec 'Great Speakers' and with quotations from original resources. His trilogy (1977, 1980, 1987) analyses the Aztecs as cultural successors to the Toltecs.

The expansion, economy and political geography of the Aztec Empire is investigated from the ethnohistorical, archaeologist's and artistic point of view by Berdan et al. (1996)

AZTEC ACCOUNTS OF THE CONQUEST

The Aztecs of Mexico were the most thoroughly observed and recorded of almost any ancient people, largely due to the efforts of contemporary Spanish priests and scribes. They wrote down accounts of history, everyday life, religion and other aspects of Aztec culture recounted to them mainly by the Aztec nobility. In these accounts, Nahuatl names, place names and other similar expressions were transliterated. The most reliable of these primary sources are Durán (1971; original 1581) and Sahagún (1950–82, 1978; original 1575–7). A later history (Tezozómoc, 1944; original 1609) was written by a descendant of Montezuma II Xocoytzin and gives a royal insider's view of Aztec history and culture. León-Portilla (1962) provides a modern reprise covering the same ground. The same author (1963) provides a classical analysis of the Aztec mentality.

SPANISH ACCOUNTS OF THE CONQUEST

Bernal Díaz del Castillo (numerous editions and translations; originally written after c. 1562) is usually taken as the definitive chronicler to both the conquest and the Aztec civilisation through Spanish eyes. Prescott et al. (1843) drew heavily on Díaz del Castillo. Cortés (1972; original 1519–c. 1526) represents a military commander's view of the campaign in Mexico, though with very detailed observations of Aztec life. However, it contains a certain amount of special pleading in the cause of the author's political struggle for recognition at the royal court in Spain. Las Casas (1965; original *c.* 1570) vividly depicts – and possibly exaggerates – the plight of the Aztecs under Spanish rule as part of the author's campaign to save the native Americans from exploitation.

RELIGION, MYTH AND ART

Burland (1967, 1972, 1980) provides a poetic understanding of Aztec religion and its deities. The same author's biography of Montezuma (1972) includes incisive accounts of Aztec religious practice and its significance. The Aztec mind, especially as revealed through art forms, is powerfully presented by Pasztory (1983), Durán (1971; original 1581), Carrasco (1992) and Taube (1993) give detailed examinations of religious rites and practices.

THE MEXICAN CODICES

The so-called Codices, the Aztec painted books, recorded Aztec history and culture in pictographic form. Most of them were created post-conquest and have been published in their origianl form, with commentaries explaining the various symbols. They include the Codex Mendoza (presently in the Bodleian Library, Oxford) (1978; original *c.* 1541/2), Ramírez (1944) and Boturini (*Tira de la Peregrinación*, 1944). The Codex Mendoza was annotated in Spanish for the elucidation of the Spanish king, Charles I.

ARCHAEOLOGY IN AZTEC MEXICO

For many years, archaeology in Mexico concentrated on the 'monumental', mainly in Mayan sites, in Yucatán or on those in Guatemala. However, since the early 1970s social archaeology has revealed a great deal about Aztec daily life and culture, and fresh sites, both large and small, are currently under careful investigation. Ignacio and Eckholm (1971) and Smith (1992, 1996–8) give detailed accounts of sites, digs and finds. Smith also provides a comprehensive overview of Aztec civilisation. A truly major discovery, the Templo Mayor in Mexico City, which was excavated after 1978, gave a boost to Aztec archaeology and is detailed in Boone (1987) and Matos Moctezuma (1988).

AZTECS ON THE INTERNET

There are numerous Web sites (mainly American) on the Internet containing a mass of information, including primary texts, some reproduced on screen in full, and details about bookshops selling both in print and out of print books. Key in 'Aztecs of Mexico'.

Index

Bold type indicates main or more significant entries